Food to LIVE FOR

We're Alive and Cooking

Recipes from the Old City Cemetery, Lynchburg, Virginia

Compiled by
Jessica Bemis Ward

Sponsored by
The Southern Memorial Association

OLD CITY CEMETERY
Founded 1806

401 Taylor Street
Lynchburg, Virginia 24501
434-847-1465
Fax: 434-856-2004
www.gravegarden.org
E-mail: occ@gravegarden.org

A Virginia Historic
Landmark on the
National Register of
Historic Places

Published by
Southern Memorial Association,
Lynchburg, VA
Design: The Design Group, Lynchburg, VA

©2013
Southern Memorial Association
Copyright is not claimed for recipes.

The Southern Memorial Association, founded in 1866, is now a non-profit, tax-exempt organization whose purpose is to manage, preserve, and interpret the Old City Cemetery, or Old Methodist Cemetery, of Lynchburg, including its graves and gravemarkers, archives, museums, and horticulture. The City of Lynchburg Department of Public Works is responsible for routine maintenance of the Cemetery.

ISBN# 978-1-938205-02-6

First printing April 2013

Notice of Rights
All rights reserved. No part of this book (except recipes) may be reproduced or transmitted in any form by any means, electronic, mechanical, photocopying, recording or otherwise without prior written permission. Information on getting permission for reprints and excerpts may be obtained from the Southern Memorial Association.

Trademarks
Throughout this book, trademarks are used. Rather than put a trademark symbol in every occurrence of a trademark name, we state that we are using the names in an editorial fashion only and to benefit the trademark owner with no intention of infringement of the trademark.

 BLACKWELL PRESS

The Speakers Belvedere, located in the center of the Confederate Section, has been a cemetery icon since it was constructed in the 1920s.

The Old City Cemetery is Alive and Well

When I first started "hanging out" in Old City Cemetery, I always brought lunch and some friends from work. It just seemed the perfect place to share a meal, conversation, and bask in the beauty of these 27 acres.

Now in my role as Executive Director, I preach the wonders of the gravegarden to everyone. We have four spheres of emphasis—cemeterial, historical, educational, and horticultural. As I like to say, if I can get you through the front gate the first time, I guarantee you will return. It is really very simple: we have something for everyone. You may only come to swing from the pecan tree or look for tadpoles and fish in the pond or stop to take in a particularly intoxicating newly opened rose blossom or get married or attend a musical event or marvel at our bee hives and goats or pay your respects to a family member or friend who "resides among us." We will be here for you and feed that part of you in need, much as the recipes in this book will bring joy, nourishment, and surprise.

Old City Cemetery is a treasure. Under the Southern Memorial Association and Jane White's indefatigable dedication, the Cemetery has been rehabilitated and continues to provide a place of wonder for our visitors. As Jessica wrote in *Food to Die For*, "Old City Cemetery was transformed into an active, happy place where people come to enjoy history and nature in what has become a magnificently beautiful spot." We are a cross section of the story of Lynchburg told in stones, plants, and a bit of mystery. Interesting programming, museums, and plantings help keep Old City Cemetery alive. Our over 15,000 residents may be quiet, but they all have stories to tell.

On behalf of the Board of Directors of SMA, the staff, and the dozens of volunteers, I invite you to come enjoy our gravegarden and see why we are the most visited historic site in Lynchburg.

—*Bruce Christian*

Table of Contents

Dedication vi

Introduction vii

    The Non-Recipe viii

APPETIZERS 1

    Baskets 7

SOUPS AND CHOWDERS 11

MAIN DISHES 21

    Letters to Save 41

A SUPPER THAT WAITS 45

A BOOK CLUB LUNCHEON 49

    Tips 53

    The Good Guest 58

MAIN DISH SALADS 63

    Minor Prejudices in the Kitchen 69

VEGGIES AND SIDE DISHES 71

    Writing the Overdue Thank You 83

SALADS 87

    Composting 90

BREAD AND BREAKFAST 93

    Housekeeping Tips 98

    Guests in the Kitchen 100

DESSERTS 103

    Favorite Things 118

APPLES 123

    Thanksgiving 133

    Afterword 136

COOKS IN THE GRAVEGARDEN 137

THE PAT MATHEWS DINNER PARTY 143

FOOD INDEX 153

Dedication

To Nancy Blackwell Marion who has been so generous with her talents, creative and practical, sophisticated and sensitive. Nancy has given us "our look." Lynchburg is lucky to have Nancy's Design Group, a homegrown firm capable of remarkable publications that rival anything produced anywhere.

To Dawn Fields Wise whose intelligence, perseverance and charm took *Food to Die For* to greater heights than any of us could have imagined.

To "Y" friends: Alex, Allison, Amanda, Andrea, Angie, Ann, Anne, Barbara, Betty, Betty, Betty, Bill, Billy, Bob, Calvin, Charles, Charlie, Cindy, Clara, Curtis, Danny, David, Dee, Duane, Earleen, Eddie, Ellen, Frances, Frank, George, Georgie, Glenn, Gloria, Gloria, Grace, James, Jasmine, Jill, Jim, Jim, Joe, Joe, Joe, John, John, John, Judy, Katie, Katie, Ken, Ken, Kitty, Laurel, Lee, Linda, Linda, Lynn, Marie, Marc, Mark, Martha, Martin, Marty, Mary, Mary Kathryn, Mary Lynn, Marinda, Maurice, Mike, Nancy, Nate, Nilson, Norma, Patricia, Paul, Peggy, Penny, Phyllis, Rachel, Renee, Robert, Sam, Sandy, Shaun, Sherri, Stephanie, Tom, Tommy, Toni, Tracy, Vickie, Walter, Wistar, Woodie, and to many other people who launch my days with good cheer but whose names are not here because of my leaky brain.

vi   Food to Live For...

Introduction

When I was gathering recipes and thoughts for *Food to Die For*, I focused on familiar foods to comfort the bereaved and to provide for those gathered for funerals. Admittedly, I also threw in a lot of favorite recipes that could be construed only very loosely as Funeral Food.

Similarly, *Food to Live For* is directed toward the foods we prepare when friends and family are gathered together. It is food for the daily meals as well as for celebrations of family and friends. This is definitely not your guide to creating extravagant menus for great and formal occasions such as weddings and milestone anniversaries. You'll need a big, hardback book for that!

This book, once again inspired by the magnificent park that is the Old City Cemetery, is designed for the meals we enjoy throughout the year. They are the family birthdays, the dinner parties for out-of-towners, the come-and-bring suppers of good friends. You will also find easy recipes to prepare for weeknights, when, perhaps, the table is set for two. Many of the recipes here are my favorite "non-recipes."

Whether you are solo or cooking for a busy household, you will enjoy your meals more if you set a table and sit down to a meal having given some forethought to presentation and composition (even if it is takeout). It will have a civilizing effect and I bet you will eat a more balanced, healthful diet.

An "old SMA" luncheon in the Confederate Section, circa 1985. Left to right: Jane White, Frances Kemper, E. Otey Watson, Jessica Ward, and Mina Wood.

The Non-Recipe

Non-recipes are my favorite recipes. Non-recipes require no set recipe. Non-recipes are simple and frequently require only salt and pepper, a little olive oil or butter, a little, or a lot, of water.

Non-recipes do require some acquaintance with the kitchen.

Non-recipes are frequently very fresh foods cooked in the simplest way in order to let foods taste like themselves!

Non-recipes are frequently inspired by a classic recipe, but not confined by it.

Non-recipes are the recipes we cook on weeknights when we open the refrigerator at 5:30 PM and see a couple of ingredients that suggest dinner. Leftover chicken and a few mushrooms suggest "Chicken a la King." I know I'll need to make a little white sauce. I don't have to get out the *Joy of Cooking* to know that I have the rest of the ingredients in my pantry and fridge.

You'll find some non-recipes in this book.

Smithsonian Institution botanist Ida Lopez and local Governor's School students took digital pictures of leaf specimens in the Cemetery as part of a nationwide research project in 2010.

Appetizers

Classic Cheese Straws

Those familiar with Food to Die For *will recognize this recipe. It appears again here for a reason: the number of ounces in the Extra Sharp Cheddar bar has been reduced from 10 ounces to 8 ounces. Before I realized that, I made cheese straws a couple of times and knew that they weren't as delicate as they should be. I hope this saves you from making that mistake since the package looks the same. You also might want to try other cheeses.*

This recipe is for a double batch. It doesn't take much longer to make the additional quantity and the straws freeze beautifully for long periods.

2 ½ Bars Cracker Barrel Extra Sharp Cheddar (20 ounces), grated

1 Pound Butter

5 Cups Sifted Flour

2 Teaspoons Salt

2 Teaspoons Cayenne Pepper

Cream room-temperature cheese thoroughly using a strong, standing mixer. Scrape down the sides of the mixing bowl several times. Add room-temperature butter and cream well for about 10 minutes or until light and fluffy.

(If possible, at this point, for shorter, tenderer cheese straws, let the butter mixture sit uncovered outside refrigerator overnight.)

Add flour, salt and cayenne pepper. Cream well again. Using a cookie press with the disk with a serrated opening, form in strips on ungreased cookie sheets. Bake at 350 degrees for about 10 minutes or until straws are blushed with brown. Watch carefully.

Tips:

- Best not to make cheese straws in high humidity.
- Whisk attachment suggested. I confess I break a whisk about once a year trying to rush "room temperature."
- Cheese, cut into chunks and brought to room temperature overnight, need not be grated.
- Straws will not brown evenly and must be watched and shifted as needed. Perhaps this would not be necessary in a convection oven.
- Straws freeze (and refreeze) beautifully for long periods.

Serves: Plenty

Al Chambers's Mother's Watercress Sandwiches

Knowing that watercress sandwiches are a favorite of Al's, I asked him how to make them. He said his recipe was very general (but aren't all sandwich recipes very general?) and these are the ingredients to play around with:

Very Thin Bread, crusts removed

2 Tablespoons Mayonnaise, approximately

8 Ounces Cream Cheese, softened, and combined with mayonnaise to arrive at spreading consistency

Worcestershire Sauce, a shake or two

2 Cups Loosely Packed Watercress Leaves (NO STEMS), chopped up (measured before chopping)

Watercress Leaves (WITH STEMS) for garnish

Mix room-temperature cream cheese, a bit of mayonnaise, some chopped watercress and a little Worcestershire sauce. Spread on bread and roll up. Tuck stemmed watercress leaves into one end of the roll for garnish. Keep moist with a damp towel 'til serving.

Now if I just knew where to find some watercress...

Pickled Shrimp

This is a favorite of the family of my cousin, Mary Carleton Young, who lives in Ft. Smith, Arkansas.

1 ½ Cups Canola Oil
1 ½ Cups White Vinegar
½ Cup Sugar
Salt
White Pepper
2 Medium Onions, thinly sliced
3 Cloves Garlic, peeled and cut in two
2 Tablespoons Chopped Fresh Parsley

4 Pounds Shrimp, cooked and shelled

Mix oil, vinegar and sugar until dissolved and add salt and pepper to taste. Combine with onions, garlic, parsley and shrimp. Marinate in refrigerator overnight, or around 12 hours, and serve with soda crackers.

Chutney Cheese Paté

This recipe used to be in every cookbook. I haven't seen it recently and so this is for the new crop of hosts and hostesses who should know about this divine appetizer. I think this is an especially good time to revive it in order to put all the great new chutneys to use.

8 Ounces Cream Cheese
1 Cup Grated Mild Cheddar Cheese
½ Teaspoon Curry Powder
¼ Teaspoon Salt
4 Teaspoons Dry Sherry
½ Cup Chutney
Green Onions

Combine first five ingredients in mixer. Shape with hands into mound on serving tray. Refrigerate until serving. Top with chutney. Snip some green onions on top.

Serve with Wheat Thins or something similar.

Watch out! It's addictive.

Cast of the Cemetery's popular "Candlelight Tours" in 2009. Every fall professional actors in period costume portray Cemetery residents by candle and lantern light.

Curry Vegetable Dip

This recipe has been with us since we lived in Richmond. It's simple and so good!

Prepare a day ahead.

1 Cup Mayonnaise

1 Teaspoon Curry Powder

¾ Teaspoon Celery Seed

2 Teaspoons Worcestershire Sauce

1 ½ Teaspoons Lemon Juice

1 Clove Garlic, minced

1 Small Onion, minced

1 Teaspoon Prepared Mustard (I use Grey Poupon or the like)

1 Teaspoon Prepared Horseradish

Combine and refrigerate. Serve with an assortment of raw veggies. Delish!

Guacamole

You may wonder why I would give you a recipe for guacamole. It's because when I make it in its stripped-down form, I get compliments. Here is simple guacamole. It's the ultimate non-recipe. My brother, Knox, trumps me in guacamole simplicity though. He says he just mashes an avocado!

1 Ripe Avocado, peeled, seeded and quartered

1 Clove Garlic, minced

¼ Teaspoon Salt (or more to taste)

Juice from a Wedge of a Juicy Lemon (or more to taste)

Two Shakes Tabasco (or more to taste)

Mash garlic and salt together. Add avocado and mash until there are no large lumps. Add lemon juice and Tabasco. Serve with pita chips or taco chips. That's it. Serves 2.

I'm so happy avocados have been declared healthy. Enjoy them before they're displaced by the next healthy thing.

Baskets

There's no doubt about it. I have baskets in excess. There is a congestion of baskets of all shapes and sizes in my kitchen. People have questioned, "Do you use all those baskets?" Yes, I do. I put several of them to work every day. And they earn their space.

Lunch Size

I take a flat bottomed Lunch Basket (about 18" long, 14" wide and 8" deep) to Kroger. It's easier for me than the cloth totes people are using to cut down on plastic and paper bags. I can tuck my Kroger card into the weave and keep coupons, recipes or a spare dollar or two under a cloth in the bottom.

When we're going to visit children and grandchildren, I designate a basket and begin, during the days before we leave, to toss things I don't want to forget into the basket.

Garden Size

A relatively narrow and shallow Garden Basket is perfect (surprise, surprise) for visiting a friend's garden where I am allowed to gather tomatoes and eggplant and Swiss chard and beets and onions and tiny green beans and… The basket is about 19" long, 12" wide and 7" deep.

Market Size

I take a Market Basket (roughly 23" long, 14" wide and 9" deep) to downtown Lynchburg to the farmers' market each Saturday. In the high season I usually nest the Garden Basket in the Market Basket as an annex for Silver Queen corn from the Saunders produce stand.

Other Sizes

We seem to be part of more and more casual, come-and-bring parties these days, and depending on the size of my offering, a Double Pie Basket (not that I'm taking two pies!) or a Casserole Basket is the perfect solution. A Small Lunch Basket (16" x 11" x 5") is more or less the same proportions at the Double Pie (22" x 15" x 5") and the Casserole (19" x 12" x 5") and the three can live nested together.

Catalogs and magazines are stashed in an open rectangular basket with handles at

Baskets 7

each end. I'm not sure what that one is called, but it's long, wide and deep.

Car Basket

There's a tall slender Car Basket (16" x 12" x 10") designed to ride on the floor of the back seat. It lives in my car trunk filled with travel essentials.

These baskets, as well as several others of different shapes and sizes, are very strong. No need to worry if they will break filled with heavy things. They mellow as they age and become more and more beautiful. These baskets have heart!

Source

Want to know where you can buy these baskets? You can call the fourth generation Gibson who makes these baskets near Fayetteville, Arkansas.

Gibson baskets are highly prized well beyond Arkansas. There have been pockets of the Gibson family making sturdy white oak baskets around the Ozarks (including the Missouri Ozarks) for several generations. We are lucky that Terry Gibson is still producing. If you watch his video on YouTube you will appreciate what a fine craftsman he is. The finished product is all white oak. No brads, no glue. And made in America!

If you call Terry at 479-443-3010, you will find for yourself what nice people he and his wife, Bonnie, are. They also have an email address: terrygibson@gibsonbaskets.com.

One of the very best features of these baskets is that they arrive by US Postal Service NAKED! Terry Gibson hangs a tag on a basket in Farmington, Arkansas, and sends it off. He has nested as many as five together, and they arrive in perfect shape on my doorstep in Lynchburg.

The Lunch Basket is the best all-purpose size and shape, but betcha can't stop with one!

Arthur, the Cemetery's resident cat, winds up in the strangest places.
Photo by Doni Guggenheimer

Members of Hillside Garden Club made a magnolia leaf horse for Garden Day, 2007.

Soups and Chowders

Chicken Taco Soup

Mary Carleton McRae, my cousin in Ft. Smith, Arkansas, says she fixes Chicken Taco Soup each year for a reunion of high school friends. She notes that it's easy to put together and can be frozen.

1 Pound Chicken Breasts, boned and skinned

2 Tablespoons Olive Oil

1 Onion, finely chopped

1 Clove Garlic, minced

1 Package Taco Seasoning

1 (15-Ounce) Can Stewed Tomatoes

1 (4-Ounce) Can Chopped Green Chiles

3 Cups Chicken Broth (or half chicken broth, half water)

1 8-Ounce Can or Jar Green Chile Salsa (adjust to taste as some salsas are very HOT)

1 (15-Ounce) Can Black Beans, drained

1 (15-Ounce) Can Pinto Beans, drained

For garnishing:

Taco Chips

Shredded Cheddar Cheese

Sour Cream

Cook chicken in seasoned water to cover. Simmer until chicken is done. Remove meat, cool and shred. In a large saucepan or stockpot, sauté onion, garlic and taco seasoning in the olive oil until onions are clear, adding shredded chicken toward the end to absorb flavors. Add remaining ingredients and cook until thoroughly heated or as long as desired. If liquid gets too low, just add more chicken broth or water. Serve with taco chips, shredded cheddar cheese and sour cream as garnishes. Freezes well.

Serves 6-8

White Gazpacho (Cucumber Soup)

This is my cousin's recipe. Barbara Ann Bemis Duke and I grew up in houses that backed up to each other in Prescott, Arkansas. She was a few years older and very glamorous. The glamor did not wear off with age. Another cousin, Maribeth Prewitt, and I were in her wedding when she married Bob Duke. We were about six. We also felt very glamorous.

Barbara Ann and Bob moved to Midland, Texas. She sent me a cookbook put together by the Museum of the Southwest there and this is one of her entries.

3 Medium Cucumbers, peeled and cut into chunks

3 Cups Chicken Broth

3 Cups Sour Cream (or 2 Cups Yogurt and 1 Cup Sour Cream)

3 Tablespoons White Vinegar

½ Cup Chopped Green Onion

½ Cup Chopped Parsley

2 Teaspoons Salt

1 Teaspoon Black Pepper, more or less to taste

2 Garlic Cloves, finely minced

For bottom of soup bowls:

2 Tomatoes, chopped

¾ Cup Slivered Almonds, toasted

½ Cup Chopped Sweet Onion

Dice cucumbers and mix in a bowl with chicken broth, yogurt/sour cream, vinegar, green onion, parsley, salt, pepper, and garlic. Pour gazpacho into bowls over tomatoes, almonds and chopped onion. Serve cold.

Serves 6-8.

Shrimp Bisque

Joan Roberson is the most resourceful cook I know. She would never rush off to Kroger mid-recipe to get an ingredient. She'd find something in her pantry that would do the trick. While she was dictating this recipe to me she was musing about substitutions. You can be certain that if she only had a white onion she would not dream of going out to buy a yellow one.

- 1 Tablespoon Extra-virgin Olive Oil
- 1 Medium Red Bell Pepper, chopped
- ½ Cup Chopped Yellow Onion
- ½ Cup Raw Shrimp, cut into pieces
- 2 Cups Half and Half
- 1 Cup Unsalted Tomato Sauce
- ¼ Teaspoon Tabasco (or to taste)
- Salt and Freshly Ground Pepper, to taste
- 1 Teaspoon Butter
- 1 or 2 Tablespoons Cognac
- ½ Cup Sour Cream (or Yogurt)
- 2 Tablespoons Snipped Fresh Chives, for garnish

Heat olive oil. Sauté bell pepper and onion until soft. Add ½ cup shrimp, half and half, tomato sauce, Tabasco, salt and pepper. Bring to a boil, reduce heat and simmer for 5 minutes. Add butter. Purée in a blender, processor or with a hand blender. Reheat if necessary, add cognac, and serve in bowls with sour cream and chives for garnish.

Serves 6.

The author's grandson Briley Ward visits one of the Cemetery's most popular attractions: a small herd of alpine goats who keep a steep hillside immaculately free of overgrowth.

Soups and Chowders

Leigh Giles's White Bean Chili

Leigh Giles has a knack for finding really good dishes that aren't too complicated. She served this one to our movie group. To qualify for Movie Group duty, a finished dish has to sit still until the movie is over. She credits her friend Ruthie Watts in Atlanta for White Bean Chili. I love recipes that are well traveled. It's a good sign.

1 Pound Dried Great Northern White Beans, soaked overnight

2 Pounds Boneless Chicken Breasts (cooked in seasoned water, to cover)

1 Tablespoon Olive Oil

2 Medium Onions, chopped

4 Garlic Cloves, minced

2 4-Ounce Cans Chopped Mild Green Chiles

2 Teaspoons Ground Cumin

1 ½ Teaspoons Dried Oregano

¼ Teaspoon Ground Cloves

½ Teaspoon Cayenne Pepper

6 Cups Chicken Stock or Canned Chicken Broth

1 Cup Monterey Jack Cheese (4 Ounces), grated

Salt and Pepper, to taste

Toppings:

2 Cups Monterey Jack Cheese (8 Ounces), grated

Sour Cream

Salsa

Fresh Cilantro, chopped (optional)

Cut cooked chicken breasts into largish bite-sized pieces.

Over medium heat, sauté onions in olive oil until translucent. Add minced garlic, the chiles, cumin, oregano, cloves, and cayenne pepper and cook for 2 minutes. Add beans and stock. Bring mixture to a boil and then reduce to a simmer. Cook until beans are tender, stirring occasionally to prevent scorching, for about 2 hours, adding a bit of water if necessary. Add chicken and one cup grated cheese and stir until cheese is melted. Season with salt and pepper.

Serve with bowls of toppings.

May be made ahead and refrigerated to point of adding chicken and cheese.

Serves 8.

Split Pea Soup

Each winter, I hope for one snow that captures us in our houses for 24 hours. Ideally, when that snow arrives, I will have the ingredients for Split Pea Soup, the perfect warming dish for looking out at deep snow. It's great with Hot Water Cornbread.

2 Quarts Water

2 Ham Hocks, with a bit of meat attached

1 Pound Bag of Dried Split Peas

2 Cloves Garlic, minced

1 Large Onion, chopped

2 Carrots, chopped

Sprig of Rosemary

Salt and Pepper to taste

In a stock pot with pasta insert, simmer ham hocks for about an hour to make a ham broth. Lift out pasta insert (it will not be returned to the stock pot), leaving the broth in the pot. Cut meaty pieces off hock to return to broth. Discard bones.

Add split peas, garlic, onion, carrots, and the rosemary sprig to broth in the stock pot. Simmer over low heat for about 30–45 minutes until peas, onions, and carrots begin to disintegrate. Add enough water to arrive at consistency that pleases you, and cook for a few more minutes. Remove rosemary sprig. Add salt and pepper to taste.

Like most soup recipes, this is better the next day, but if it's snowing outside . . .

Serves 6.

P. S. Learn from my experience. I cooked pea soup early in my married life, and when I was leaving the kitchen after supper, the pot of soup was still very warm and I decided that, given the ingredients, I would not refrigerate it. BIG mistake. When I came down next morning, there was a terrible odor. I checked all possible offenders. Then the lid on the soup pot rattled! My soup had fermented and was breathing like the monster from Planet X! Of course it had to be thrown away. It took me a winter or two to regain my yearning for pea soup.

Soups and Chowders **15**

Crawfish (or Shrimp) and Sausage Chowder

Here's a recipe from my friend, Carolyn Terry, who lives in Magnolia, Arkansas. She gives credit to a caterer, Kathy Gean, for this delicious chowder. Unfortunately, I live too far from crawfish territory to be able to get fresh crawfish, so I have used shrimp.

4 Ounces Andouille Sausage, diced

1 Tablespoon Butter

1 Onion, diced

1 Red Bell Pepper, diced

2 Stalks Celery, diced

1 Teaspoon Dried Thyme (or a Tablespoon Fresh Thyme)

Salt and Pepper, to taste

3 Cups Whole Milk

3 Cups Frozen Shoepeg Corn, thawed

3 or 4 Medium Red Potatoes, cut into ½" dice

1 Pound Crawfish (or 1 Pound Shelled Shrimp)

1 Cup Cream (or Half and Half)

Sauté sausage, butter, onion, red bell pepper, celery, thyme, salt and pepper in a stockpot over medium heat, about 10 minutes. Add milk, thawed corn, potatoes and crawfish and simmer until potatoes are tender—about 35 minutes. Stir in cream and heat gently.

Serves 4–6.

Ellen's Sausage Chowder

One day last winter, Ellen Petty said she had a recipe she thought I'd enjoy. She was making chowder for a family gathering and brought me the recipe along with the proving pudding. She was right! It's delicious! And with Ellen's canned shortcuts, it's off-the-shelf simple. Mid-winter you'll be writing Ellen love letters.

1 Pound Bulk Sausage

1 Large Onion, chopped

1 Stalk Celery, sliced

1 Green Pepper, chopped

1 Clove Garlic, minced

Butter or Oil for sautéing

2 16-Ounce Cans Kidney Beans

2 14-Ounce Cans Stewed Tomatoes

2 Cups Tomato Juice

1 Bay Leaf

1 ½ Teaspoons Seasoning Salt (or more to taste)

1 Teaspoon Chili Powder

½ Teaspoon Dried Thyme

¼ Teaspoon Pepper

1 Can Corn

Sauté onion, celery, green pepper, and garlic in a little butter or oil in a large Dutch oven. Remove from pan and brown sausage. Mix sautéed vegetables and sausage with remaining ingredients and heat.

Serves 6–8.

Soups and Chowders **17**

Corn Chowder

Our niece, Aanjes Larkin, several years ago sent a small collection of her very favorite recipes as a Christmas present. This delicious Corn Chowder recipe was among them.

3 Ears Corn, shucked

1 Pound Potatoes (I used Yukon Gold), cubed, but left unpeeled

2 Quarts Water

1 Teaspoon Salt, more to taste

1 Medium Onion, chopped

1 Tablespoon Olive Oil

1 Tablespoon Flour

1 Red Bell Pepper, chopped

2 Sprigs of Thyme

2 Bay Leaves

3 Cups Heavy Cream

3 Scallions, finely chopped

½ Teaspoon White Pepper

⅛ Teaspoon Cayenne Pepper

Chopped Cilantro

Cut corn from cob, then hold cob upright in bowl and scrape with knife to extract "milk." Reserve cobs. Bring water to a boil and add cobs, potatoes, and ½ teaspoon salt. Return to a low boil and cook until potatoes are done—about 15 minutes. Discard cobs.

Meanwhile, sauté chopped onion and ½ teaspoon salt in the olive oil in a large heavy pot over medium heat, stirring occasionally, until onion is pale golden—about 10 minutes. Add flour and cook for 2 or 3 more minutes.

Add bell pepper, corn and its milk, thyme and bay leaves. Reduce heat and cook, covered, stirring occasionally for 15 minutes. Stir in potatoes with their cooking water and cream, and simmer until reduced to about 7 cups—about 30 minutes. Stir in scallions, white pepper, cayenne pepper, and salt to taste. Discard bay leaves and thyme sprigs. Garnish with cilantro.

Serves 8.

Lynchburg artist Anne Adams Robertson Massie captured the author and E. Otey Watson in the Confederate Section on Memorial Day, 1990.

The antique rose 'Pink Summer Snow' blooms in profusion on the old brick wall, just outside the Cemetery Center.

Main Dishes

First in this section are five chicken dishes. They're all delicious. Two are casseroles. A chicken casserole may not be twenty-first century chic, but sometimes a chicken casserole is a necessity when, Yikes, you've got too many things going on. You find yourself with company coming on the heels of a busy day. Resort to a reliable chicken (chicken is so versatile and isn't apt to cause problems for anybody except vegetarians) dish. As so many articles advised us in the sixties, you'll have the satisfaction of being able to spend time with the guests you've invited. Believe me, food snobs may pass judgment, but then they will eat.

The first recipe was to have been Club Chicken, a recipe given to me years ago to cook for a Sweet Briar Day luncheon. I remembered it being very good but when I cooked it with an eye to using it in this book, all I could think was, "This reminds me of Chicken a la King, and I wish it tasted more like Chicken a la King." So I concluded that I should instead just give you the recipe for Chicken a la King.

Chicken a la King

- 2 Cups Diced, Cooked Chicken Breasts
- 1 Cup Sliced Mushrooms, sautéed in butter
- ¼ Green Pepper, diced and sautéed with mushrooms
- ¼ Cup Diced Pimientos (2-Ounce Jar)
- 4 Tablespoons Butter
- 4 Tablespoons Flour
- 2 Cups Chicken Stock/Cream (You can use either or a combination)
- 1 Egg Yolk, slightly beaten
- Salt and Pepper, to taste
- 1 Tablespoon Dry Sherry

Melt butter in heavy saucepan. Whisk in flour and cook 3 or 4 minutes, stirring frequently, to remove flour-y taste. Slowly add broth and/or cream, whisking until sauce is smooth and has just begun to boil. Lower heat and add chicken, mushrooms, green peppers and pimientos. Whisk in egg yolk. Season with salt and pepper. Stir in the sherry before serving over rice or toast.

Serves 4.

Children of Cemetery Superintendent Clement R. Woodall, Jr., enjoy the snow outside the old Caretaker's House which used to be located in the Earley Memorial Shrub Garden. (photo circa 1955)

Chicken and Green Chiles Casserole

The second dish is one that is sometimes referred to as the King Ranch Casserole. I love Helen Corbitt's version of this, which is not made with canned soup. Many versions are. This came from Helen Corbitt Cooks for Company.

6 Large Chicken Breast Halves, cooked and cut into bite-sized pieces

4 Tablespoons Butter

1 Cup Chopped Onion

3 Tablespoons Flour

2 Cups Milk

1 Cup Chicken Broth

1 4-Ounce Can Green Chiles, seeded and cut into strips

1 10-Ounce Can Rotel Tomatoes

5 6-Inch Corn Tortillas, torn into bite-sized pieces

¾ Pound Sharp Cheddar Cheese, grated

Melt butter. Add onions and sauté 1 minute. Add flour and cook until bubbly. Pour in milk and broth and cook until thickened, stirring frequently with a whisk. Mix green chiles with the sauce. Add Rotel tomatoes. Place a layer of chicken in buttered shallow 3-quart casserole, then a layer of tortillas, cheese and sauce. Repeat, reserving some cheese for top. Bake at 375 degrees until bubbling. May be frozen.

Serves 10.

Main Dishes **23**

Lisa's Non-Recipe for Chicken

Our daughter-in-law, Lisa, served delicious chicken breast pieces one night recently. She guessed at the formula, which follows. Feel free to be fairly casual about the proportions and achieve a fine result.

6-8 Boneless, Skinless Chicken Breast Halves, each cut into 3 or 4 pieces

Marinade:

1 Jar Stonewall Kitchen Wasabi Mustard

¼ Cup Orange Juice

1 Tablespoon Red Wine Vinegar

2 Tablespoons Olive Oil

Stir marinade ingredients together. Pour over chicken several hours before cooking and refrigerate. Grill.

Serves 6-8.

P. S. The chicken does not taste like any of the marinade ingredients. It is just moist and delicious.

P. P. S. Don't worry too much if you can't find wasabi mustard. Dijon mustard will be fine.

Chicken Curry

This is simple enough for a weeknight supper. It is winning enough, especially with the addition of lots of condiments, to be used for a dinner party. The original recipe came from a cookbook, The Helen Corbitt Cookbook, first published in 1957. The streamlined classics in that collection continue to be recipes I've returned to ever since.

I've modified the recipe over the years, frequently adjusting to what I have in my refrigerator. I have reduced butter and omitted cream. And I do one thing not in the original recipe. I add chopped apple to the onions and celery sautéed at the start of the recipe. And one time, when I didn't have a fresh apple, I slipped ½ cup applesauce into the sauce.

Curry Sauce

½ Cup Chopped Onion

¼ Cup Chopped Celery

1 Peeled, Chopped Apple

¼ Cup Butter

½ Teaspoon Salt

1 Tablespoon Curry Powder (more or less to taste)

¼ Cup Flour

3 Cups Milk (or half milk, half chicken stock)

1 Cup Half and Half (or more milk)

2 Tablespoons Sherry

3 Cups Cooked Chicken (or what you have) cut into large dice

Sauté onions, celery and apple in the butter until onions are yellow; add salt and curry powder and mix thoroughly; add flour and cook until bubbly. Add milk and chicken stock, stirring until smooth and thick. Helen Corbitt says to cook until the starchy flavor has disappeared.

Here are the accompaniments she suggests:

Chutney

Diced Crisp Bacon

Finely Diced Hard-cooked Egg Whites and Yolks, diced separately

Finely chopped Salted Peanuts or Pecans or Almonds

Finely Chopped French Fried Onions

Shredded Coconut, fresh if possible

Shredded Bombay Duck (an Indian fish delicacy)

A Tart Jelly

Finely Chopped Sweet Pickles

Pappadums (a special wafer from India)

French-fried Shrimp

Olives, ripe and stuffed

Seedless Raisins

Cheesey Chicken Casserole

In the mid-seventies, my sister-in-law, Anne Stern, compiled a family cookbook. It is a treasure and I return to it again and again for familiar recipes. In addition to supplying many good recipes, it is as good as a photo album to reveal the array of personalities in the Ward family.

This recipe is from Dorothea Ward Gilfoyle. Dorothea's chicken entry in the family cookbook is a bit different from the ones with similar ingredients that were de rigueur at every sixties dinner party. No mushroom soup! I have updated it only by barely blanching (rather than thoroughly cooking) the broccoli before layering. Like many recipes we abandoned during the eighties and nineties, this is worth returning to.

6 Chicken Breasts

2 10-Ounce Packages Frozen Broccoli
(or equivalent amount fresh)

2 Cups Milk

2 8-Ounce Packages Cream Cheese

2 Teaspoons Salt

2 Cloves Garlic, minced

2 Cups Cheddar Cheese, grated

Gently simmer chicken breasts in seasoned water until just tender. Remove skin and bones. Cut into bite-sized pieces. Blanch broccoli. In a double boiler, blend milk, cream cheese, salt, garlic and ¾ cup cheddar cheese. Cook and stir until smooth. Put broccoli, cut into bite-sized pieces, into a lightly greased 2-quart casserole. Add a layer of cheese sauce. Add the chicken. Cover with rest of cheese sauce. Sprinkle remaining cheddar cheese on top and bake at 350 degrees for about 25 to 30 minutes until piping hot.

Serves 8-10.

Salmon with Lemon

When Betty Jo Hamner gave me the marvelous Tomato Pie recipe (which you can find in the Veggies and Side Dishes section of this cookbook), she told me she had another current favorite recipe. I knew it had to be good! This recipe doesn't sound as good as it is. You'll be missing a great one if you don't try it!

2 Vidalia Onions, sliced
4 Salmon fillets
Olive Oil
1 to 2 Lemons, sliced thin
Fresh Rosemary

Preheat oven to 425 degrees. Make a bed of half the sliced onions in the bottom of a greased baking dish. Place salmon steaks, skin side down, on top. Brush salmon with olive oil. Arrange sliced lemons on top of salmon. Snip rosemary over lemons. Place remaining onions on top of all. Cover and bake for about 20 minutes.

The Walton family of Chesapeake, Virginia—direct descendants of Claiborne and Amelia Pride—visited the Cemetery in 2011.

Main Dishes **27**

Cold Salmon and Good Sauce

Like the Cheesey Chicken Casserole, this dish is from Anne Stern's family cookbook. Her sister Dearing credits her good friend Gene Dahmen as the source of this recipe for Cold Salmon and Good Sauce. The recipe for poaching the salmon is sketchy: "Poach salmon in water with wine, bay leaf and pepper for about 15 minutes." That moves me to add that it took years into my cooking career to realize that liquid for poaching is simply water, but flavored so that the result is not a watery-tasting chicken or fish. Don't get too uptight about precise measurements. I'll make up some here, if it makes you feel better.

Cold Salmon

Good Sauce

1 Clove Garlic

4 Tablespoons Capers

4 Small Green Onions

1 Tablespoon Worcestershire Sauce

1 Teaspoon Salt

1 Teaspoon Pepper, freshly ground

1 Egg Yolk, beaten (optional, if you're worried about uncooked eggs)

1 Teaspoon Lemon Juice

1 Teaspoon White Vinegar

1 Cup Sour Cream

1 Pint Mayonnaise

4 Tablespoons Chives

8 Teaspoons Dried Parsley (or 1 Cup of Fresh Parsley, chopped)

1 Tablespoon Dried Tarragon (or 3 Tablespoons Fresh Tarragon, chopped)

Place filleted salmon in a fish poacher or other vessel of a shape to accommodate a whole piece. Ideally, the salmon will rest on some sort of rack to make removal easy. Feel free to improvise. Add just enough water to cover. Pour in a half cup white wine or dry Vermouth. Add six or eight peppercorns. Add a teaspoon of salt (sea salt, if you have it). Add a bay leaf, if you have one. Add a sprig of fresh parsley, if you have that.

Simmer salmon on top of stove or in oven (depending on which is best for the shape and composition of your cooking vessel) for about 15 minutes. Remove from liquid and cool. Serve with chilled Good Sauce.

Good Sauce

Mash garlic, capers and green onions together to make a paste. Dearing advises that this "takes a long time." It has dawned on me that you could accomplish this with a food processor (that no one possessed in 1976). The sauce can now be done in less than a minute. Anyway, add Worcestershire sauce, salt, pepper and egg yolk. Add lemon juice and vinegar. Mix well, then add sour cream, mayonnaise, chives, parsley and tarragon and pulse several times. At this point, Dearing interjects that "this makes a lot." That's good, because you can have it again in a few days.

Refrigerate and use with cooled salmon.

Shad Roe

I can't remember when I had my first taste of Shad Roe. There certainly weren't a lot of shad in Southwest Arkansas! I must have been encouraged to try it on my first trip to Virginia when I was ten. I loved it and have ordered it whenever I've found it on a menu since. At first I thought it was Shad Road which was forever after how my family referred to it.

I learned how to cook it, though I have to relearn every spring. The trick is to cook it thoroughly without drying it out. Here are three suggestions for cooking to perfection:

1. The Rappahanock Fish Market in Richmond had recipes on slips of paper that called for wrapping each side of a set of shad roe in a slice of bacon. The roe is then packaged in waxed paper and secured with a toothpick. The package is cooked in a skillet over moderately low heat until the bacon has browned—a sure sign that the shad is done. Mine has sometimes been a little too done.

2. Linn Ong passed on a recipe from James Beard which aims at preserving the moisture with a little less trouble. He recommends melting butter in a skillet over low heat until the butter has just begun to form tiny bubbles. Add shad, cover and continue to cook for 12-15 minutes, turning once. Season with salt, pepper and chopped parsley.

3. Actually Beard should have cooked bacon in the skillet first and cooked the roe in a little of the bacon grease left after the bacon had been removed. You must have bacon with shad roe. It's the law. Serve roe and bacon on toast, which extends the taste of both.

Lobster Dinner

For a number of years, members of the Kiwanis Club in Lynchburg have sold live lobsters driven down from Maine as a fundraiser. Signing on for a dozen lobsters has frequently been the kick-start I have needed to invite friends to dinner. Serving lobsters is one of those pleasures, like camping out, which calls for logistical planning and results in a colossal mess, but is worth it.

As a general rule, I don't welcome guests' help in the kitchen. However there are times when I really, really need it! Sharon Ainslie offered, and I accepted, help with my inaugural lobster bout. I'd never cooked lobsters and needed the support of experience to have the nerve to plunge the poor things into boiling water. I will always be grateful for her practical help as well as her reassurance.

Buck Bradley, good soldier that he is, has also come to my assistance with lobsters more than once. Like Sharon, he is a stalwart ally in the midst of chaos.

Here are some hints I'll share after gaining late-life lobster cooking experience:

- Boil as much salted water in as many large vessels as you can fit on the top of your stove!

- Boil the lobsters for 15 minutes—one year I undercooked. Whoops!

- The lobsters come packed in seaweed. Throw that into the boiling water for flavor.

- Supply lobster crackers for each guest. If you haven't enough, ask your guests to bring any they might have. Use those oyster forks you've had lying in wait in your silver drawer for 40 years. They're perfect for getting into the little spaces.

- Prepare for a BIG mess:

  - Invite guests to wear the same clothes they would wear if they were going on an ocean voyage in a small, open boat. In a storm.

  - Use a plastic cloth to protect your table. I have a plastic-laminated Marimekko cloth that gets a little stiffer every year, but it still does the trick.

  - Supply multiple napkins for each guest.

  - Supply bibs for each guest.

- Remove the lobsters from the boiling water to colanders so they can drain a bit. Ellen Petty says she cracks each lobster in a couple of places for draining.
- Don't worry too much about what else you're having. The main event doesn't allow for attention to much else. Provide a side plate for whatever accompaniment you serve because it gets swamped if it has to share a plate with the lobster. Serve bread sticks—which don't take commotion to heat or serve.
- Place trash cans with heavy-duty bags near the table and get them out of your house as soon as possible.
- Prepare to smell like ocean and fish. Hmmm. Maybe we'll get a steamer.

I have often thought that if I had to kill my food, I'd be a vegetarian. Cooking lobsters is the only case where I have been the killer. It has been reported that the experience of being put into boiling water is not painful for the lobsters. Explain to me, then, why they're resisting the experience so violently.

Old City Cemetery is a popular spot for bridal and wedding photographs.
Photo by Allegra Helms

Main Dishes **31**

Deviled Crab in Shells

I've found myself reaching back to old solutions for what to serve guests. One thing we've abandoned for the last couple of decades is deviled crab in shells and it's a pity. It's easy to prepare, can be made ahead and presentation in natural scallop shells is easy and fun. I wish I could tell you that this is also inexpensive, but I can't. This is when you start espousing "Time is money" and "It's less expensive than eating out."

Although there are recipes for deviled crab involving white sauces and many ingredients, I am most likely to turn to Deviled Crab in Shells when I don't have a lot of time to prepare. In addition, I don't want so many ingredients that the delicious sweetness of fresh crab meat is obscured.

1 Pound Lump Crab Meat

⅔ Cup Mayonnaise

1 Teaspoon Dry Mustard

1 Tablespoon Lemon Juice

4 or 5 Drops of Tabasco Sauce

¼ Cup Sweet Onion, finely minced (optional)

Mix ingredients. Fill buttered shells, place on a cookie sheet and bake in a preheated 325-degree oven for 25 to 30 minutes.

Fills 4 shells lavishly, 6 adequately.

Shrimp Cooked in Beer

Don't worry too much about precision in the proportions, or even the ingredients, in this recipe for cooking shrimp. The object of this recipe is to get the shrimp cooked in a flavorful broth. It is not designed to arrive at beer-tasting shrimp. You will not detect beer in the finished product.

2 Pounds Raw Shrimp, with shells on
2 12-Ounce Bottles of Beer
1 Clove Garlic, peeled
1 Teaspoon Salt
2 Bay Leaves
1 Teaspoon Celery Seed
A Sprig of Parsley
A Pinch of Cayenne Pepper
Juice of Half a Lemon

Bring beer and all of the listed ingredients except shrimp to a boil. Add shrimp, reduce heat and cook for about two or three minutes until shrimp are just turning pink. Shrimp may need to be stirred a bit so that all shrimp are cooked. Try not to overcook.

Chill shrimp. Serve with a mixture of melted butter, lemon and Tabasco, or with your favorite cocktail sauce. Or use in any other way you would enjoy cooked shrimp.

Each diner can peel his own shrimp at the table. This makes an easy and festive summer supper when served with a substantial side dish and some good bread. Don't forget to provide a "boneyard" on the table for the shrimp shells!

Serves 4.

Main Dishes **33**

Spaghetti with Shrimp and Spicy Tomato Sauce

I asked Bruce Christian, director of the Old City Cemetery, if he would ask his wife, Spas, for the recipe for one of his favorite dishes. Here it is, and now it's one of my favorites too!

1 Pound Spaghetti

1 Pound Raw Shrimp, peeled

5 Tablespoons Olive Oil, separated

4 Cloves Garlic, chopped

½ Teaspoon Red Pepper Flakes

1 Pint Cherry Tomatoes, halved or quartered (or better yet, homegrown tomatoes in season)

1 Roasted Red Pepper (if doing your own roasting) *or* 1 or 2 Jarred Roasted Peppers

Salt and Pepper

⅓ Cup Cilantro, chopped (or more to taste)

Cook pasta in boiling water until al dente. Drain in a colander and toss with 1 tablespoon olive oil.

Sauté shrimp in 4 tablespoons olive oil over moderately high heat in a 12-inch skillet. When shrimp turn pink, remove shrimp and add garlic and pepper flakes to oil. Sauté until garlic is fragrant—this happens *quickly*!

Add tomatoes and roasted red pepper and cook over moderate heat just until tomatoes begin to lose their shape—about 5 minutes.

Season sauce with salt and pepper. Return shrimp to pan, add pasta and toss for a minute to thoroughly mix.

Remove from heat, add cilantro and toss again.

Serves 4.

Mina's Tuna Steak

Mina is a great cook who is more often guided by what's in her refrigerator than by any recipe. This applies to cooking a tuna steak, which, as you can see from Mina's suggestions, should spare you another trip to the grocery store! Her son, Marshall, who is also an accomplished cook, has basic advice, which is to get a fairly thick tuna steak (an inch or more thick) and marinate it for an hour or more. Add salt and pepper and cook it in a hot skillet on top of the stove or on the grill for five or six minutes on each side. The goal is a pink, but not raw, interior. Some people like it raw. If you're one of them, cook it for a shorter time!

Here are Mina's suggestions for marinades: soy sauce, lemon juice, lime juice, orange juice, maple syrup, brown sugar, bourbon . . . and I'm sure she would not want you to be confined by that list. You can also use one of the many bottled marinades.

Whatever you do, make sure to cook enough tuna so you can make Mina's liberated Nicoise salad in the Main Dish Salads section.

Beloved Cemetery resident "Blind Billy" led our Bicentennial Funeral Parade in 2006. The parade stretched for five blocks!

Main Dishes **35**

Beef Stroganoff

Beef Stroganoff was one of those dishes hostesses discovered in the sixties. It was easy to make with uncomplicated ingredients, improved by being prepared ahead and was almost always well received. It was an ideal dish and so it became "used up" as a menu option. When it was first served to me in 1963 by another young bride, it seemed very sophisticated—especially when served with a large jug (with potential for becoming a lamp) of cheap red wine.

Our friends Elsie and Bill Chambers invited us to supper the other night and Elsie served the following recipe that she'd made the day before. It was delicious and satisfying on a cold February night. Elsie passed along the recipe. I have tacked on a couple of options used by Helen Corbitt in her Stroganoff recipe from her cookbook written in the sixties.

3 to 6 Tablespoons Olive Oil

1 ½ Pounds Sirloin Steak or Tenderloin, trimmed of fat and cut in strips

2 Tablespoons Flour

1 Cup Sliced Mushrooms

½ Cup Thinly Sliced Onion

3 Cloves Garlic, minced

3 Tablespoons Butter

4 Tablespoons Flour

2 Tablespoons Tomato Paste

1 Can Beef Broth

1 Cup Sour Cream

Salt to taste

½ Teaspoon Caraway Seeds (optional and not in Elsie's recipe)

Dash of Nutmeg (also optional and not in Elsie's recipe)

2 to 3 Tablespoons Dry Sherry (optional and Elsie opted not to use it)

Thin Egg Noodles

Heat oil in skillet. Shake meat in plastic bag with 2 tablespoons flour and 1 teaspoon salt. Brown meat and remove from pan. Add more oil as necessary and sauté onions and mushrooms until they begin to brown. Add garlic and cook for 3 more minutes. Remove onions, mushrooms and garlic from pan.

In the same pan, melt 3 tablespoons butter, mix in 4 tablespoons flour and 2 tablespoons tomato paste. Add beef broth and stir until smooth and thick. Add meat, mushrooms and onions. Reduce heat, stir in sour cream and warm gently. Do not allow to boil. Add sherry if desired. Serve on cooked noodles.

If you choose to make the Stroganoff ahead, you can refrigerate just before stirring in the sour cream.

Serves 6.

Shepherd's Pie

If you have enjoyed the easy and delicious Tomato Bouillon in Food to Die For *you'll want to try this recipe, also from Laura Sackett.*

Mashed Potato Topping:

7 Medium Potatoes (about 2 Pounds)

⅔ Cup Milk, warmed

2 Tablespoons Grated Parmesan Cheese

12 Ounces Lean Ground Beef or Lamb

1 Large Celery Stalk, finely chopped

1 Medium Onion, finely chopped

½ Teaspoon Dried Thyme Leaves

½ Teaspoon Dried Oregano

1 Pound Carrots, peeled and cut in half lengthwise and then into ½" chunks

1 ½ Pounds Medium Mushrooms, quartered

1 Small Bag Frozen Tiny Peas, thawed

Salt and Pepper

Optional:

Sharp Cheddar Cheese, shredded

Paprika

Peel and cook potatoes. Mash to desired consistency with heated milk and Parmesan cheese. Add salt and pepper to taste.

Cook ground meat, celery, onion, thyme and oregano until meat has browned. Save juices in pan. Move mixture to plate with slotted spoon. In same pan, sauté carrots and mushrooms until tender. Layer in casserole: meat mixture, carrots and mushrooms, and peas. Spread mashed potatoes on top.

If desired, sprinkle sharp cheddar and paprika on top of the potatoes.

Bake in a preheated oven at 425 degrees until potatoes are golden brown.

Serves 8-10.

Note: Make mashed potatoes however you usually make them, assuming you do! Laura says she sometimes buys the already made potatoes at the supermarket.

The proportions of veggies to meat in this dish didn't sound right, but it was delicious. I served it to company recently. I think they didn't think they were going to like Shepherd's Pie but they went back for seconds.

Asparagus and Eggs au Gratin

Here's a good brunch dish. Also good for Sunday night supper. Definitely retro, but not as much when using fresh asparagus rather than the canned asparagus originally called for. My family served this when I was growing up, and the recipe was also included amongst those that Peter's aunt, Lucy Irvine, collected for me when Peter and I were married. We served this for a wedding breakfast for Peter's sister, Dearing. When Dearing and TR were married, we were living at "Ricohoc," Lucy's farm near Evington. It seemed just right on a Saturday in the country and tasted mighty good with Smithfield ham biscuits. Can't remember what else we served, but it must have been fruit in some form.

1 Large Bunch Asparagus, lightly steamed (or you can use the 2 cans of asparagus spears called for in the original recipe if you really want to go retro)

5 Eggs, hard boiled and sliced

4 Tablespoons Butter

4 Tablespoons Flour

2 Cups Milk

½ Cup Cheddar Cheese, grated

1 Teaspoon Salt, or to taste

A Grind of Pepper

Preheat oven to 350 degrees. Melt butter, add flour and cook for a minute or two. Slowly add milk, whisking all the while to make a smooth white sauce. When thickened, remove from heat and add the cheese, salt, and pepper. Pour over the asparagus and egg slices that have been layered in a baking dish. Top with bread crumbs and bake in oven until slightly bubbly and until the asparagus seem cooked. You can stick the asparagus with a fork to be sure they're cooked enough.

Serves: 4

Melanie's Shitake Mushroom and Prosciutto Pasta Dish

Melanie Christian is a delightful, energetic person who can be counted on to be fully involved in the many projects she undertakes. She is a good cook who seems undaunted by large numbers. And she and her husband, Lynch, have a spacious house which they generously often open for one group or another. It's always a treat to be there and there's always good food. Here's an example:

2 Cups Onion, chopped

1 or 2 Garlic Cloves, minced

1 Pound Shitake Mushrooms, sliced*

1 Teaspoon Dried Oregano (or 1 Tablespoon Fresh Oregano)

1 Teaspoon Dried Basil (or 1 Tablespoon Fresh Basil)

2 28-Ounce Cans Italian Tomatoes

¼ Cup Butter (½ stick)

2 Tablespoons Flour

2 Cups Milk

¼ Cup Prosciutto, cut into pieces

¼ Cup Fontina Cheese, grated

¼ Cup Gorgonzola Cheese, crumbled

1 Cup Parmesan Cheese, grated

½ Cup Parmesan Cheese, grated

Fresh Parsley, chopped

1 Pound Bowtie Pasta

In a skillet, sauté onion in a little olive oil. Add garlic and sliced shitakes and continue to sauté. Add oregano, basil and canned tomatoes to the mixture.

In another pan, make a white sauce by melting butter, adding flour and stirring over medium heat for 3 or 4 minutes. Stir in milk and whisk until the sauce has thickened.

Add prosciutto, fontina, gorgonzola and 1 cup of parmesan to the sauce and stir to mix.

Cook bowtie pasta according to package directions until al dente. Mix everything together and transfer to buttered baking dish. Top with the remaining ½ cup Parmesan cheese and parsley and bake at 350 degrees until the dish is heated through and parmesan has melted.

Serves 8.

*Three ounces dried shitakes weigh approximately one pound when reconstituted by soaking in hot water for 30 minutes.

Marion Farmer's Quick Red Beans and Rice

Marion Farmer is a good cook who grew up in Poplarville, Mississippi, not very far from New Orleans, which comes through in the personality of this recipe.

¾ Pound Smoked or Andouille Sausage

1 Tablespoon Olive Oil

1 Cup Coarsely Chopped Onion

½ Cup Chopped Green Bell Pepper

½ Cup Chopped Celery

2 Cloves Garlic, minced

¼ Teaspoon Freshly Ground Black Pepper

½ Teaspoon Dried Thyme

½ Teaspoon Dried Basil

½ Teaspoon Creole Seasoning (optional)

Salt to taste (Canned beans have considerable salt, so add at end)

3 15-ounce Cans Red Kidney Beans, undrained (Marion uses organic)

¼ Teaspoon Tabasco or Cayenne Pepper

Worcestershire Sauce, to taste

1 ½ Cups Rice, uncooked

Parsley and Green Onions for garnish

Cut the sausage into ½-inch pieces and put all ingredients except the beans, Worcestershire, Tabasco and rice, into a deep (4 quart) ovenproof casserole, cover and heat in a 325 degree oven until vegetables are soft, about ½ hour. Stir in the beans, along with Tabasco and Worcestershire sauce, cover again and cook until they are somewhat mushy. Check to see that they don't dry out; you may need to add ½ cup water or more. In a separate pot, prepare 1 ½ cups rice according to package instructions while the beans cook. Add salt and additional pepper if needed. Serve the beans over rice with chopped parsley and chopped green onion for garnish.

Marion suggests that "you can put the rice in an attractive shallow serving container, put the beans on top, garnish with chopped green onions and chopped parsley, and let guests serve themselves. For a simple supper, you can served the rice and beans in individual bowls with French bread on the side. "

Serves 6–8.

Letters to Save

I have a box in which I keep a few very special letters. These are letters that are so remarkable in some way or other, no matter who the writer, that I feel compelled to save them. Yes, the feelings about the writer or the special message delivered in some of them makes them more saveable, but in general I put them in the box because they are superb examples of their missions.

I have a letter written by a neighbor as thanks for food after a tragic death in her family. It is such a warm, dignified, connecting letter, that I always read it before setting about that task myself. Her thoughtful choice of words left me feeling valued as a friend.

Another very, very short note is from a young woman whom I will probably never see again. She's now divorced from my connection with her. But she wrote a thank you for a baby present that was remarkable because it was so brief and yet it accomplished its purpose so charmingly. Pay attention all you very busy young mothers! Here's what the note said: "Thank you so much for the baby bonnet for Cynthia. I can't wait until we come to Lynchburg so she can meet you." And that was it! I've had many letters from many people who felt obliged to fill every space on the note paper which didn't accomplish what that note accomplished.

And while I'm on the subject of short, our friend Gena sent a postcard after supper here recently. All she said was, "It was perfect. Absolutely perfect." What hostess would not bask in that short—and perfect—message. When I think of that note, it inspires me to invite people over. Especially Gena and Bill! I should hasten to add that the meal wasn't perfect, but it seemed perfect because we had such a good time with our perfect guests.

I have another letter that I've saved with a transcription because the handwriting in the letter from the charming, elderly person who wrote it is shaky and almost illegible. It was worth figuring it out though. She is regretting that she could not be at our relative's funeral. "My thoughts and prayers are with you. I am sorry, indeed, that I am now in a more or less immovable state, having no car to drive, and legs that refuse to perform except for the shortest distances. Otherwise I would have been at your side to show you my real feelings: sadness for our families that another wonderful member has been taken from us, and distress for you that you must now face each day without her. I know that—and so I send you my love, as always, and my very deep and heartfelt sympathy." I wasn't going to include the whole of that, but I just didn't know where to stop. It's moving even if you don't know the cast of characters.

My box has many letters. But alas, I'm afraid my collection of superb examples will probably never outgrow the box. And it can't all be blamed on email.

SMA officers Jane White, Mina Wood, Frances Kemper, and Jessica Ward greeted visitors at the dedication of the Pest House Medical Museum in 1988.

Emily Patton Smith led a Botanical Illustration Workshop in 2011.

Visitors lay fresh evergreen wreaths on veterans' graves every December during the Cemetery's annual Wreaths Across American ceremony.

A Supper That Waits

For a number of years, several couples have gotten together once a month on Sunday nights to watch a movie. Ideally, the movie is one that is a gem that might have been missed by the local theaters. Or by us. Sometimes it is a classic oldie. Although the guidelines for choosing a movie are loose, generally the movie is meaty enough to provoke conversation at dinner. There have been many great movies, some good movies and a few bad ones.

Over the years, the TV sets have gotten wider and flatter, the homes have gotten smaller, and the meeting times earlier, but members, supplied with drinks and popcorn, still happily crowd in together to watch a movie in improvised living room theaters.

Supper follows the movie. Movie quality may vary, but supper is always superb! The original mandate was that supper be very simple. Although hostesses have strayed a bit from "simple," one thing that is necessarily constant is that the meal be one that survives the movie. A Supper That Waits. It is frequently a one-dish meal, such as soup or a casserole that can be prepared ahead, plus a salad.

One thing that has stayed simple is dessert. Generally a brownie or a Dove Bar suffices.

Jocelyn and Tom Connors have moved to Winston-Salem, but Jocelyn has shared one of her more recent dinner menus and recipes. It revives memories of happy times and great meals at their house in Lynchburg.

Jocelyn's Chicken Country Captain for Movie Group

8 Boneless, Skinless Chicken Breast Halves

½ Cup Flour

1 Teaspoon Salt

Pepper, to taste

½ Stick Butter

¼ Cup Olive Oil

1 Large Onion, chopped

2 Medium Green Peppers, chopped

2 Cloves Garlic, minced

2 14.5-Ounce Cans Diced Tomatoes

1 14.5-Ounce Can Tomato Sauce

2 to 3 Teaspoons Curry Powder

½ Cup Raisins

1 Package Slivered Almonds, toasted

Chopped Parsley

Hot Cooked Rice

Chutney

Cut chicken into bite-sized pieces (she uses scissors). Combine flour, salt and pepper in a bag and use to coat chicken pieces. Brown chicken in butter and olive oil in large skillet. Remove to baking dish with slotted spoon. Add onion, green peppers and garlic to skillet and sauté. Add tomatoes, tomato sauce, curry powder and raisins. Simmer for about 10 minutes. Pour over chicken. Cover baking dish and bake at 325 degrees for 1 ½ hours. Garnish with almonds and parsley. Serve with rice and use chutney for accompaniment.

Serves 14–16.

Jocelyn's Pear and Apple Salad

Here is Jocelyn's perfect accompaniment for Chicken Country Captain.

Combination of Salad Greens, such as Spinach, Romaine and Red Leaf Lettuce

1 Gala Apple, not peeled, cut into small pieces

1 Red Bartlett Pear, same as for apple

½ Cup Toasted Walnuts

3 to 4 Ounces Crumbled Blue Cheese

Balsamic Dressing:

Make Good Seasons Italian Dressing, using canola oil, balsamic vinegar and a little more water than in directions.

Tear greens into bite-sized pieces. Just before serving, toss with Balsamic Dressing. Sprinkle apple and pear pieces, walnuts and blue cheese on top.

Jocelyn's Brownies from Scratch

Brownies are about as elaborate as Movie Group desserts ever get. Jocelyn's, from scratch, were delicious.

1 Box (8 Squares) Baker's
  Unsweetened Chocolate

2 Sticks Butter

5 Eggs

3 Cups Sugar

1 Tablespoon Vanilla

1 ½ Cups Flour

1 6-Ounce Package Nestle's Semi-
  sweet Chocolate Chips

½ Cup Chopped Walnuts or Pecans

Preheat oven to 350 degrees. Melt chocolate and butter. Set aside to cool a bit. Put eggs, sugar and vanilla in mixing bowl and beat on high for 10 minutes. Add chocolate/butter mixture and continue beating. Slowly add flour and mix until thoroughly blended. Add chocolate chips and nuts.

Bake in a large buttered 9" x 13" pan for 40-45 minutes. Let cool before cutting into squares.

P. S. I always begin to check doneness about 10 minutes before baked goods are supposed to be done.

A Book Club Luncheon

I belong to three book clubs. That's two too many, but I like them all and don't want to withdraw from any one of them. Thank heavens they read some of the same books! And thank heavens I can listen to some of the books on my iPod!

By and large, refreshments for the monthly meetings are simple: Coffee, tea and soft drinks, easy snacks, and sometimes a coffee cake at the one that meets on Monday mornings.

For the last meeting of the year in May, the Monday morning club hostess frequently chooses to do a luncheon. The three recipes that follow comprise a menu that Lydia Daniel served and that I thought particularly appealing. I remember the wonderful aromas of spinach casserole and spoon bread that greeted us when we arrived.

Lydia was kind enough to write the recipes out. Lydia's aspic is different from the one from Marianne Rhodes in *Food to Die For*, but equally good. It has evolved over the many years in Lydia's kitchen. I think she told me that the original recipe came from *Joy of Cooking*. Didn't all recipes?!

Lydia Daniel's
Canned Tomato or Vegetable Juice Aspic

2 Tablespoons (or 2 envelopes)
   Unflavored Gelatin

8 Cups Canned V-8 Juice

1 Cup Clamato Juice (You can skip
   this and use 9 cups V-8)

½ Cup Seafood Cocktail Sauce

Lemon Juice, to taste

Optional:

1 to 2 Cups Celery, chopped

1 Cup Canned Artichoke Hearts,
   chopped

Soak the gelatin in ½ cup room temperature V-8 Juice. Mix the remaining V-8 Juice, the Clamato Juice, and Cocktail Sauce. Add softened gelatin mixture. Add lemon juice to taste. Pour into ring mold and chill. When the aspic is chilled and about to set, add celery and/or artichokes as desired. Chill the aspic until firm.

Lydia advised serving with Hellman's mayonnaise. Homemade mayonnaise would be an extra treat. She also suggests filling the center of the aspic ring with marinated cucumbers or avocados, chicken or shrimp salad, or cottage cheese and chives.

Serves 8.

Lydia Daniel's Spinach-Artichoke Casserole

This, too, is a bit different from the Spinach-Artichoke Casserole in Food to Die For.

2 Boxes Frozen Chopped Spinach, drained and squeezed

1 Stick Butter

1 Tub Whipped Philadelphia Cream Cheese

1 or 2 Chicken Bouillon Cubes, according to taste

1 Can Artichoke Hearts, drained and chopped

Salt and Pepper, to taste

Cook (undercook) the spinach with the butter, cream cheese and bouillon cube until ingredients are melted and blended. Add artichoke hearts and mix well. Salt and pepper may be added to taste.

Pour into buttered casserole dish and heat in 275 degree oven until piping hot.

Serves 8.

Lydia Daniel's Spoon Bread

Lydia Daniel's Spoon Bread is Washington Old Fashioned Spoon Bread Mix. She follows the directions on the package. FYI, you'll need milk and egg!

Serves 8.

The "Soulsters from the Hill" choir of Diamond Hill Baptist Church participated in a church history walking tour of the Cemetery in 2003.

Tips

Most important tip for good cooking

Marry someone who eats everything, even your mistakes, with relish. Also marry someone who is willing to go out to dinner when your mind stalls at the thought of cooking supper. The freedom to cook anything (or not anything) will make putting a meal on the table a lot more fun. And you will do more of it, and get better at it.

Tips for hosts and hostesses

Anytime you have more than six people, consider using place cards. They don't have to be prissy place cards, but designating places helps to assure that couples don't stay glued together. It allows the hosts to place guests so that each can be comfortable. So each can shine.

When arranging seating for a large dinner, such as a wedding reception, use the place cards themselves to move around to plan the seating. Once the arrangement has been made, stack the place cards for each table in the decided-upon order and tuck the cards into a plastic bag. A bag for each table.

A good way to get started planning seating for a very large group, assuming you're making an effort to mix everyone up, is to divide the place cards into categories. For example: Family, Prospective In-Law Family, College Friends, Childhood Friends—you get the idea. Begin to pluck one from each category for each table. Granted, there are some combinations that won't work, but this will get you launched and then you can make adjustments.

Display a seating chart at the entrance to the dining room so that each person can determine where he/she belongs without touring every table.

Little tips

Use tape, such as Scotch Magic tape (the kind you can write on), to mark reusable freezer or refrigerator containers with contents and date. You can peel it off and refill and re-mark over and over.

Tips **53**

When using votive candles, put a tablespoon or two of water in the bottom of the votive cup before inserting candle. The spent candle will be MUCH easier to remove and replace. Or place the votive cups in the freezer for 20 minutes or so and the wax will become brittle enough to crack out.

Kosher salt and most of the gourmet sea salts can't be sprinkled from an ordinary salt shaker. Here's one solution: Reclaim an empty spice jar—one with its top perforated to accommodate larger bits—for easier sprinkling of salt granules. And make it a project to find shakers with larger holes. I have an Italian pottery one I bought years ago that works fine.

For those of you who are so busy with young families that you feel you can't use your flat silver because you can't put it in the dishwasher, I've got good news. You CAN use it. True, dishwasher-washed silver doesn't have the same gleam. But when the children have flown and you have a little more time to hand wash silver, you can restore the glow with a polishing or two. Our wedding silver survived twenty five years of dishwasher washing just fine and I have the memories of a quarter-century of family meals using it. And yes, I have hollow-handled knives, and they too went in and out of the dishwasher many times. I choose to hand wash now and there seems to be no ground lost in appearance in spite of years of Cascade.

An aside: Dish washing. It's one of my favorite household jobs, probably because it's finite. There aren't many jobs that are finite. You start with very definite soil and end up with very definite clean and in a relatively short time. I find it very satisfying.

Tips from friends who are extraordinary hosts

The following tips are from friends who are great cooks who entertain frequently. You'll notice that the advice is generally to make putting good food on the table simpler, easier. As my friends and I age, none of us wants anything to be so complicated that it becomes an obstacle to having friends in.

Betty's tip: Even if you are having a catered party, you need to serve one homemade dish to put your signature on the party.

Gena's tip (the flip side of Betty's tip): When you are preparing the food yourself, you need to have at least one dish that you don't cook. Bring in the dessert, side dish or main dish already prepared. Reduce the chaos.

54 Food to Live For...

Gena's tip #2: Serve a Drive-Around dinner: When the alternatives are taking guests out, bringing in dinner (or, heaven forbid, not having company), this is a good solution. Gena has some favorite foods to pick up. Fried chicken from one spot, potato salad and slaw from another and dessert from a third.

Duane's tip: Repeat a successful menu over and over. Presumably it's something you like and the preparation of the meal gets easier and easier. Even guests who are invited back can look forward to your delicious, signature menu. My friend Linn endorses this practice.

Betty's Tip #2: Have a party in the freezer at all times. At the very least she tries to keep a cake and a loaf of her homemade bread.

My own tip: Keep some no-fuss nibbles on hand to serve with drinks. I keep cheese straws in the freezer and Trader Joe's Roasted Marcona Almonds with Rosemary in a tin. The almonds taste even better if you roast them a bit more.

Here's a great suggestion from Marion Farmer: Instead of sautéing the usual ingredients (chopped onions, garlic, celery, etc.) for beginning a sauce, soup or stew, she pops them into a covered, enameled iron casserole with butter or olive oil and heats in an oven at 250 until they are soft. No vigilant stirring. No fine spray of oil to cover the kitchen. No strong odors.

Plant the herbs you use in abundance. Overabundance. Otherwise, when you have your salmon out and spot one tiny plume of dill, you're probably going to have the instinct to SAVE the dill for another time. Then it will go to seed and you'll NEVER use it.

So plant more parsley, thyme, chives, tarragon, basil, oregano, and dill than you can possibly use. Almost all herbs make agreeable companions to other garden plants and parsley makes a refreshing row against a wall. I've planted herbs in the drainage chinks in a retaining wall. You can stuff them in and they don't seem to suffer. Jane White adds that herbs add lovely texture and a variety of green to a flower border.

You can also plant a pot full of herbs. Really full. In my experience, you can keep nudging them in tightly. I keep a large pot of herbs at my back door. I've never had much luck bringing potted herbs into the house, though, in spite of all the cute little pots of windowsill herbs you see advertised.

You can root many herbs, among them, rosemary, basil and thyme. When you've clipped more than

Tips **55**

you need, put the surplus in water on your windowsill, and when they've sprouted some roots, stuff them into the herb pot.

When you're having a dinner party, set the table ahead. You can accomplish that even a day or two in advance. It is a head start that stays put and is psychologically reassuring as you face the jobs that need to be done closer to party time.

When you're setting the table for a party, start with the plates. It makes it easier to establish the spacing.

Meal planning tips

People seem to stall on "what to have for dinner." See if you don't find that this helps: Have a couple of default meals each week. For instance, Monday nights I generally try to use something already in the house. It might be leftovers or something from the freezer. Unless we've been away for the weekend, there's usually something in the refrigerator that inspires a meal. I can build on a bit of chicken or black-eyed peas or salad greens. I could be well on my way to one of Mina's Lynchoise salads (page 67).

The default meal on Tuesday nights is salmon. The fish has just come in after the weekend and we look forward to a favorite meal. And I don't have to ponder what to have.

You're on your own for the rest of the week!

Leftovers

When a number of leftovers have accumulated in our refrigerator, we have a "Week in Review" smorgasbord at our house. The foods and wines are a hodge podge and would make any serious foodie cringe. But we enjoy this way of dealing with the leftover dilemma.

Recently many of our leftovers have been rescued by our wonderful Bedford Avenue Meat Market in Lynchburg. Along with the very best meats, chicken, cheeses and salads, they have whole wheat pizza shells. Add dibs and dabs from recent meals and you have your leftovers reincarnated.

Other cooks deal with leftovers in different ways. Marion Farmer says that she freezes small amounts of leftovers with the intent of making a "scrumptious" soup. The soup is different every time but it is yummy to mix all those flavors: beans, pasta, rice, tomatoes, potatoes, spinach, squash, different types of stocks and meats. She says, "Sometimes I make a cassoulet instead. The great thing is, you don't

56   Food to Live For...

have to start from scratch when you get ready to make the soup or cassoulet; everything is in your freezer ready to be assembled."

And here's a suggestion from our daughter-in-law, Lisa: Add grated cheese and bits of leftover chicken or meat to tortillas to make quesadillas. Our three grandsons love leftover night!

Rose lovers browse the rooted rose cuttings for sale at the Cemetery's Annual Antique Rose Festival in 2004.

The Good Guest

Much is made over being a good host or hostess. There are many books written on how to provide food to company with apparent ease—even if that food has been a week in progress. A host couple feels an obligation to provide a festive setting—whether simple or elaborate—including flowers, music and a congenial choice of guests. Good food and drink are important. The host and hostess are ready to greet each guest warmly and introduce any guests who have not met. The aim of the host is to make every guest feel welcome and comfortable.

Too little has been written about the guest's responsibility to help assure the success of a gathering. Thinking of accepting an invitation as making a contract with the hosts to help make the party "work" may seem a bit severe. But one should definitely attend with an attitude of active participation. And this does not necessarily mean leaping up from the table to clear plates. It has more to do with helping make the shared time a happy occasion for everybody there. Including the host and hostess. For starters, this means that the arriving guest does not find and cling for the rest of the evening to the most familiar people in the room. We all have been at gatherings where close friends cluster and have a conversation that, by its nature, excludes others. That conversation should be carried out on the phone the next day.

A conversation should be expandable to include people who join the group. The nature of the conversation should be relayed in a few words to new arrivals, who may actually have something to add to the subject.

A most valued guest is one who can be counted on to circulate and even take on stray guests. I can remember early in our marriage that I always felt secure when our friends Mary and Jack Spain were on the guest list because they could be relied upon to move around and talk to everybody, including Peter's grandmother who could no longer do her own circulating. The Spains are my archetypal "good guests." They have done interesting things themselves (including a multi-month Marco Polo trek) and are eager to find out interesting things about others.

Jane White says that being a good guest is just good manners and is the natural consequence of being considerate of others. Unfortunately, most people are self-conscious, and yes, a little anxious, when entering a room full of people, and that frequently stands in the way of mixing around to make a party "work."

Here's a tip for your next outing. Arrive at the party with the intent of finding out the best things about someone there you might not know very well and allowing that person to shine. If you feel like you are ready for the varsity, take on someone considered difficult, because they are dull or aggressive or peculiar. Make a project of having a good conversation and discovering interesting things about the person. I bet you'll find a person under there you never expected. With luck there won't be more than one of those people at a thoughtfully concocted party, though!

Here's something I've discovered relatively recently about conversation starting. First of all, don't begrudge having a sentence or two about the weather or the traffic—the low gears of conversation. I've found a good question that's a key to opening up real talk is, "What did you do today?" Even if they raked the yard and went to Kroger you can talk about gardening and food! You could strike a conversational gold mine like, "I was awakened this morning by a call from the Nobel Prize Committee." But what's more apt to happen is that the person will tell you what he did not get to do. That will give you a clue to real interests.

I was talking about this express route to finding out about someone you don't know well with Barbara Harbison. She said why don't you just ask them what they didn't get to do today that they wish they'd been able to do! I'll have to try that, though asking them what they did, which is easily answered assuming they didn't spend the day watching a naughty TV channel, allows them to ease into the interesting stuff.

At the same gathering, Danny Garza, who lives in New York City, said he hates being "chatted up." When conversation becomes a duty without any underlying interest, I guess that's what happens. One hopes that there is some curiosity about other people's concerns and lives that is genuine and can foster a good give and take. That having been said, don't count on having a conversation where you touch bottom every time you have a social experience. Some of my very best talks have come in odd places and without benefit of alcohol. Try the Harris Tire Company waiting area! Martha Miller and I were there one day while we waited to have our cars' oil changed. We had what I consider one of my top-ten conversations of all time.

Here's a tip the hosts can use to enliven a party. Throw in at least one couple who mixes things up a bit. It doesn't have to be someone with controversial views necessarily, but just someone whose views aren't known. Someone not among the usual suspects. The mystery guests will save the group from falling into a conversation rehashed from many parties before. Conversations circulated amongst peo-

The Good Guest 59

ple we see all the time can get pretty consolidated.

Sadly, it is the nature of people to get less expansive about making new friends as they get older. This is not all bad, because sometime one just yearns to nurture longtime friendships. But with age comes the loss of friends and sometimes a narrowing of interests. Making new and younger friends helps avoid the focus on self that comes as lives get limited in one way or another. Adjusting to new friends refreshes.

Being the good guest does not mean that you have to be a Chatty Cathy or Charles. So what if you are not the quotable Mr. Bon Mots! You can be the good guest by mixing with more than your best friends, by making a point to find something interesting in another guest. Make it a project. I know it sounds Pollyannish, but you're probably up for some surprises.

Cemetery docent Lynn Stuart demonstrates the Civil War-era "dental key" tooth extractor in the Pest House Medical Museum.

The swing has been the Cemetery's most popular spot since 2000.

Photos courtesy of (clockwise, from top left) Kale Golden, Melissa Markham, Dolly Pugh, Blaine B. Bush, and Stephanie Yonce

Main Dish Salads

Paella Salad

Here's another fabulous recipe from my friend Linn Ong. She has given me many of my favorites. Since we live beyond entertaining range of each other, I use her recipes freely.

This is a delicious, gorgeous main dish salad. It is colorful and makes an impact when served fully garnished on a large platter. Only bread is needed to complete the meal. Or you could serve toasted pita triangles with hummus. I have also found that pimiento cheese sandwiches made with thin sliced Pepperidge Farm bread seem to go well with the salad.

3 or 4 Cups Cooked, Shredded Chicken

2 Pounds Cooked, Peeled Shrimp

2 Italian Sausages, sliced and sautéed (Optional)

¼ Cup Olive Oil

2 Cups Long Grain Rice, Uncooked

3 ½ Cups Hot Chicken Broth

Pinch of Saffron

1 Cup Sliced Celery

Frozen Peas, Defrosted, Not Cooked (Optional)

½ Cup Minced Onion

6 Tablespoons Minced Cilantro and/ or Parsley

Garnishes: Quartered Tomatoes, Romaine Leaves, Roasted Peppers, Lime Wedges, Pimiento-stuffed Olives

Dressing:

¾ Cup Olive Oil

4 ½ Tablespoons Balsamic Vinegar

1 Teaspoon Curry Powder

1 Teaspoon Dry Mustard

¾ Teaspoon Salt, or to taste

½ Teaspoon Pepper

Heat ¼ cup olive oil in a heavy, 3-quart enameled casserole. Over moderately high heat, add rice and stir constantly until *light* brown. Dissolve saffron in hot broth and add to rice. Cover and cook until done. Blend the dressing and add half of it to still-warm rice. Add chicken, shrimp, vegetables and herbs to rice mixture. Add remaining dressing and chill for an hour or two. Garnish.

Serves 10.

Orzo Salad

This superb recipe came from Jackie Humphrey. She brought her Orzo Salad to Betty Harris's beach house one summer for a Girls' Weekend and everyone went home with the recipe! Here it is:

16 Ounces Orzo

1 Tablespoon Olive Oil

1 or 2 Cloves Garlic, minced

1 10-Ounce Package Fresh Spinach, washed and trimmed

6 Ounces Kalamata Olives, quartered

8 Ounces Feta Cheese, crumbled

4 Ounces Sundried Tomatoes, in oil, drained and cut into strips

Salt and Cracked Pepper, to taste

While orzo is cooking, heat skillet. Cook garlic in oil for 20 seconds. Add spinach and cook 2 minutes until wilted. Drain, put into bowl. Add olives, feta and tomatoes. Mix well.

Drain orzo and put back in pot to evaporate water. Add spinach mix.

Jackie suggests that adding a few thinly sliced spring onions would be nice, although the salad she brought was delicious without them.

Serves 6.

Cemetery beekeeper Luther Weiland explained the secret life of bees during a program in 2002.

Greek Salad

I am so picky about my salad greens that I don't like to make salad! But when I bite the bullet and prepare one, there's nothing I like better than a salad. I only make this salad when tomatoes are at their very best in mid-to-late summer.

When I begin a Greek Salad, I always wonder if it will be enough. But by the time I've piled up all the goodies on top of fresh, crisp romaine, I stop wondering. It's a full, satisfying meal. A little hummus with toasted pita goes nicely.

This recipe is more or less from the recipe book of Greek food that came as an offer from the Krinos company. I now use the ingredients here, plus a few others from the olive bar at the grocery. I generally add dolmas (stuffed grape leaves) to the platter.

2 Heads Romaine, tired or leathery outer leaves discarded

2 Summer Tomatoes, cut into wedges

1 English Cucumber, peeled and thinly sliced

½ Red Onion, very thinly sliced (the Krinos recipe calls for scallions)

5 Radishes, thinly sliced (I never seem to have radishes)

½ Cup, or more, Pitted Calamata Olives

¾ Cup Feta Cheese, cubed or crumbled

8 Anchovies (we like more)

Dressing:

½ Cup Olive Oil

¼ Cup Wine Vinegar

1 Tablespoon Lemon Juice

1 Teaspoon Salt

1 Tablespoon Chopped, Fresh Oregano (or 1 Teaspoon Dried)

Tear washed greens into bite-sized pieces. Place on large platter. Sprinkle with some of the dressing. Add tomatoes, cucumber, onions and radishes. Add dressing as needed. Garnish with olives, feta and anchovies.

Serves 4.

Main Dish Salads **65**

Jane White's Crab and Caper Salad

For the multitude of you out there who have tried and loved Jane White's Corn Pudding in Food to Die For, *here's another of her recipes. She found it in a cookbook called* Something to Talk About *from Darien, Georgia. It's sure to be the perfect centerpiece for an uncomplicated and delicious summer meal. The lump crabmeat is very expensive, but you can think of the outlay this way: how much you're saving by eating at home!*

1 Pound Fresh Lump Crabmeat

1 4-Ounce Jar Capers, drained

1 Cup Mayonnaise

½ Cup Vidalia Onion, finely chopped (more or less to taste)

Juice of One Lemon

Mix and chill.

Serves 4.

Jane told me that this is simply wonderful. As usual, she was right. A perfect meal was created by adding Smithfield ham rolls (Jane has a secret source for divine homemade rolls), tomato aspic and Jane's Corn Pudding. For dessert, she served Marzipan Cake (also in *Food to Die For*) with vanilla ice cream and sliced peaches.

Mina Wood's Nicoise (or Lynchoise) Salad

I saw Mina in our Kroger produce department yesterday where she was shopping for organic lettuce for a Nicoise Salad. She was planning to use grilled tuna from the previous night's supper. She says she buys extra tuna from the Blue Marlin (our wonderful local fish market) with the second meal in mind. I asked her for her Nicoise formula, which she emailed me with the disclaimer, "I am a casual cook so here is what I think I do." Actually, Mina is a talented and resourceful cook able to make inventive use of what she has on hand. I've been eating and admiring her cooking since we were both young brides in Richmond and she was turning out delicious meals when I was struggling with the basics.

Her first advice was to make sure that all the tuna steaks are the same thickness. She says that she grills the tuna so that it is beyond rare, but still pink inside. She recommends peeking to see if the steak has arrived at the right degree of doneness. She suggests cutting the tuna across the grain into thin slices to put atop the salad.

Mina says I should look up an authentic Nicoise recipe. I'll let you do that. She says she simply puts some or all of the following ingredients on a bed of any kind of salad greens. She mentioned romaine and spinach, but also et cetera, so take your pick!

Sectioned Tomatoes
Black Olives
Anchovies
Hard Boiled Egg Wedges
Sections of Roasted Potatoes
Cooked Green Beans
Grilled Tuna

She drizzles the composed salad with a balsamic or lemon vinaigrette.

My guess is that Mina has arrived at the exact spirit of the salad produced by cooks in Nice who want to refresh leftover ingredients.

Soloists Joseph Carson, Sarah Hoffman, Mark Howell, and Emily Howell performed 19th-century music during a "Bransford Vawter Day" concert in 2006.

Minor Prejudices in the Kitchen

I don't use garlic salt. When a recipe calls for garlic salt, I just add a little minced garlic and a little salt. Garlic salt tastes fake to me. Not using it means one less bottle to store and keep fresh.

If I'm going to eat fat, I want to spend those fat calories on butter, not margarine. I use a lot of olive oil instead of butter now. I even use it on my Irish Oatmeal. I used a 50/50 combo of butter/olive oil for a while and then switched to olive oil entirely.

I now eschew the recipes that call for canned soup. Some of the recipes are wonderfully good and I enjoy them at other people's houses. I guess I've just gotten where I want to be a little more in control of my ingredients—even when some of them are not a particle better for me!

I want impeccable greens for salads. I would never pour out a batch of greens from a so-called ready-to-eat bag and use it unsorted and unwashed. I'm a fanatic in respect to salad greens. It's why I hate making salads, but why I love eating them. I'm amazed at how many restaurants serve weary greens.

I love Balsamic vinegar, just like everybody else in the world. It's as ubiquitous as ketchup and actually may be the upscale counterpart. People put Balsamic vinegar on everything. Too much, I'm afraid. Everything tastes like Balsamic vinegar. It's so in, it's bound to go really out. Where has it been all the years? I don't think I ever heard of Balsamic vinegar until the early nineties!

Hill City Master Gardeners often share the magic of compost with school groups at the Cemetery's Compost Education Center.

Veggies and Side Dishes

Scalloped Tomatoes

This is a superb recipe from Lamar Cecil. It's richly, deeply sweet. Lamar and his wife, Geri, are superb hosts, undaunted by large numbers. They live and entertain in a daringly, fabulously decorated house. They always serve great food. The fact that Lamar has included quantities for expanding the recipe to serve 80 should tell you something about his pleasure in being a host. Here's his recipe for Scalloped Tomatoes just as he sent it via email.

1 28-Ounce Can Whole Tomatoes (Del Monte are the best but any brand will do.   Do NOT use equivalent of fresh tomatoes), juice reserved

1 Medium Onion, chopped

⅓ Green Pepper, chopped

8 Strips Bacon, cooked, with fat retained

3 Stems Celery, chopped

3 or 4 Slices White Bread, torn into small thumbnail-size pieces

¾ Cup Juice from Canned Tomatoes (retain remainder)

½ Cup Packed Dark Brown Sugar

1 Tablespoon White Vinegar

Salt

Pepper

Lea & Perrins Worcestershire Sauce

Fry bacon in an iron skillet. Remove when brown and crumble when cool. Leave bacon fat in skillet. Sauté the onion, green pepper and celery in the bacon fat until limp. Crush the tomatoes over the skillet with your hands and add the ¾ cup tomato juice. Then add the bacon, bread pieces, the sugar and vinegar. Add salt, pepper and Lea & Perrins to taste and correct the sugar and vinegar combination to whatever degree of tart/sweetness you desire. The mixture at this point will be somewhat soupy. Place it in a greased 9 x 13-inch Pyrex dish. Bake at 350 degrees for approximately 45 minutes. Check consistency after 30 minutes or so. What you want is a consistency that is like cornbread dressing—damp but not runny. If the mixture seems too dry, add some of the tomato juice you have retained. If it's too runny, cook it a little longer. This is best served hot but if your oven is crowded it is fine at room temperature. It can be multiplied as many times over as you desire.

Serves 8.

Lamar adds: To feed 80, I use 8 28-ounce cans of whole tomatoes, and proportionate amounts of bacon and vegetables, 2 cups brown sugar, 6 tablespoons vinegar, etc.

Stewed Tomatoes

Here's Jane White's recipe for stewed tomatoes:

"I chop up fresh or use many cans of chopped tomatoes, no skin. Use a big hunk of butter, some oregano, pepper, and cook it down. Towards the end, I add a tablespoon of sugar (and a tablespoon of salt if the tomatoes are fresh) and keep cooking 'til it's right."

Here's mine using canned tomatoes:

Sauté one chopped onion in a couple of tablespoons of butter in a skillet. Add bread crumbs that have been made by whirring a couple of slices of bread in a processor. Sauté until onions are translucent and crumbs are just beginning to brown. Add a large can (28-ounce) peeled, diced tomatoes. Add a little sugar, about a teaspoon, and salt and pepper to taste, and stew until slightly thickened. No herbs here. Serve in a saucer so it won't invade every other thing on your plate.

Serves 4.

Summer Vegetable Casserole

This recipe was inspired by "Fresh from the Garden Casserole," in Good Cookin' from the Heart of Virginia. *That superb cookbook, first published in 1985 by the Junior League of Lynchburg, is no longer printed.*

This recipe was from Perkins Flippin. Much good food came from her kitchen at Pharsalia in Nelson County. This is a great example of her solution to mid-summer bounty.

I urge you to use this recipe as a mere suggestion, as I did. When I did not have all of Perkins' ingredients, I used what I had. I still do, and the resulting casseroles are different and delicious every time.

Slice thinly, any or all of the following vegetables:

Small Firm Zucchini

Small Firm Yellow Squash

Small Firm Pattypan Squash

Fresh Ripe Tomatoes

Mild White Onions

Sliced Green Bell Pepper

Additional ingredients:

Salt and Pepper

Thin Slices of Butter

Minced Fresh Thyme

Lemon Juice (from a couple of wedges)

Topping:

Grated Cheddar Cheese

Layer thin slices of the vegetables, adding a little salt, pepper, butter, and thyme, and a squeeze of lemon every couple of layers. Top generously with cheese and bake in a pre-heated 350-degree oven until vegetables are cooked as you like them.

P. S. Perkins' recipe called for McCormick's Lemon 'n Herb Seasoning, which I didn't have when I first came across this recipe. I've never bought the Seasoning, and just add a little lemon juice and thyme instead. She also did not include bell peppers. Suit yourself. You, too, will probably make some changes. Get back to me when you do!

Veggies and Side Dishes **73**

Lisa's Delicious (and Easy) Summer Squash

Our daughter-in-law, Lisa, has supplied me with some of our favorite daily recipes. She and Pope have three young sons, so you know that on the average weeknight she's not doing anything very complicated. She has found that the key to winning young palates to healthy food is to serve fairly straightforward dishes. Here's just such a recipe that uses the summer's abundance of zucchini, yellow and pattypan squash. This is one of those non-recipes that I love.

Olive oil

Summer Squash (Zucchini, Yellow or Pattypan), sliced ¼-inch thick into rounds

Salt and Pepper

Parmesan Cheese, optional

Preheat oven to 425 degrees. Using a baking pan with one-inch sides, skim the pan with olive oil. Tilt the pan until completely covered. Add sliced squash. Flip squash so that both sides have been "oiled." Add salt and pepper. If desired, add a sprinkling of Parmesan. Bake until the squash begin to brown and sizzle. That should take about 30 minutes, but check after 20.

One pan (10" X 15") can accommodate 3 or 4 sliced squash—enough for 2 or 3 people.

Tomato Pie

This is one of those dishes that you remember. It was memorable even in a standout meal. It was so good that I feared maybe it was a secret dish. It's the kind of recipe you couldn't be blamed for keeping to yourself. I decided it was such a good recipe that I would try to get it for this book. I need not have worried. Betty Jo Hamner generously shared. You may have seen recipes for Tomato Pie but none to equal this. As soon as next summer's tomatoes are ripe, before you make the first BLT of the season, make this!

1 Deep Dish Pie Crust, brushed with butter
1 Tablespoon Floor
1 Onion, sliced
Several Large Tomatoes, peeled and sliced
1 to 2 Cups Fresh Basil Leaves
¾ Cup Mayonnaise
2 Cups Cheddar Cheese, grated

Pierce pie shell in several places with a fork. Bake until light brown. Remove from oven and sprinkle with flour. Place onion slices in pie shell. Heap tomato slices on top of onions. Top tomatoes with fresh basil. Mix mayonnaise and cheddar and spread over all. Bake at 350 degrees for about 30 minutes or until the vegetables have become tender.

Serves 6 to 8.

Director Emerita Jane Baber White is a passionate advocate for old roses.
Photo by Doni Guggenheimer

Veggies and Side Dishes **75**

Black-Eyed Peas

Here are Jane and Kenneth White's separate directions for cooking black-eyed peas:

First Kenneth, just as he sent it:

"It doesn't rise to the level of a 'recipe.' I just dump the peas in a pot with water, then dump in some bacon grease, beef bouillon, red pepper (lots) and salt and pepper. No measurements and so it never comes out the same.

"Jane won't eat it."

And Jane:

"This is hilarious. I must say this is exactly what Kenneth does, which is why I cannot eat them if he makes it, but I do like my own version which incorporates much less red pepper. Sad to say, the heaping tablespoon of bacon grease is important. We have always used fresh black-eyed peas from the market, which are extremely expensive, so I honestly don't know how to do it from soaked dry."

And my formula isn't so far off theirs:

First, I make a bacon broth simmering a half-inch chunk of dry salt pork in about three or four inches of water. You could use half a slice of bacon if you don't keep salt pork. Let the broth brew for about half an hour until about half the water is gone. Don't let it boil away! You can guess I have!

Add a pint of fresh black-eyed peas, a half teaspoon of salt and some grinds of black pepper, and cook about 30–45 minutes until they're firm but done. Underdone, even though a cooked consistency has been reached, can still taste a little raw. You'll know. Just taste.

And adjust the seasonings. Sometimes I throw in a halved jalapeno, not for heat, since I remove the seeds, but for that delicious flavor.

Cooked black-eyed peas freeze well. Make sure liquid covers them in the freezer container. Comforting food on a cold night.

Delicious Simple Beets

My friend Duane Nelligan has great kitchen instincts. She is resourceful and loves to try new things. Her recipe for roasted beets is a current favorite of hers—and of all the people who enjoy food at her house.

It falls within that wonderful category, non-recipe, so don't get too concerned about proportions here. These directions are her estimates.

4 Bunches Small Beets (if larger than a ping pong ball, cut in half)

1 or 2 Large Sweet Onions

Olive Oil

Salt to taste

Optional: Rosemary or Thyme

Preheat oven to 400 degrees.

Cut tops off beets (saving tops to sauté later if you want) and scrub. Cut top and bottom off beets, but don't peel. Peel and cut onions into wedges.

Mix beets and onions in a large bowl. Toss with a generous amount of olive oil. Add salt (and rosemary or thyme). Line baking pan with parchment or foil and pour mixture into pan. Roast for about 30 minutes. Start checking for "fork tenderness" after about 20 minutes.

Recipe expands and contracts easily.

Carrot Souffle

For those of you who are familiar with Food to Die For, *you'll probably remember that I am an admirer of Leigh Giles's recipes and menus. I've paid her the sincerest compliment over and over by asking for and publishing her recipes. Here's another from her that is unusual and unusually good. As with all of Leigh's recipes, it is not complicated. You don't even have to divide the eggs! This is a snap if you own one of those hand-held blenders which allow you to purée without transferring to a processor.*

I halved the butter and sugar and really didn't feel that it affected the delectable goodness of this recipe. Double the amounts given here if you'd like to try the original. Or omit the butter altogether if you're keeping track of those things!

1 Pound Bag "Baby" Carrots
¼ Cup Butter (½ stick)
¼ Cup Sugar
1 Teaspoon Baking Powder
3 Tablespoons Flour
3 Eggs
½ Teaspoon Salt, or more to taste
1 Teaspoon Pure Vanilla Extract

Preheat oven to 350 degrees. Cook the carrots in salted water in a large saucepan until tender. Drain carrots and add butter and purée in a processor or with a hand-held blender until smooth. Combine the remaining ingredients in a large bowl and mix thoroughly. Add carrot mixture to egg mixture and mix well again. Add more salt, if needed.

Pour mixture into a 1 ½-quart greased baking dish and bake about 40 minutes. Serves 4–6.

Potatoes au Gratin

This is a recipe that you generally have all the ingredients for. If you have potatoes (baking or new), onions, milk, cheddar cheese, and a little butter, you can combine them, skipping the white sauce step, to make a delicious side dish. This is ideal to save a skimpy meal when you want to avoid a trip to the grocery. It falls into the category of non-recipe—my favorite category!

Potatoes, scrubbed but unpeeled, sliced thin

Onions, sliced thin

Butter

Flour

Sharp Cheddar, grated

Milk (any strength!)

Salt and Pepper

Place a layer of sliced onions in the bottom of an oven-proof casserole. Put a layer of sliced potatoes on top of that. Dot with thin slices of butter amounting to about a teaspoon for a small casserole. Sprinkle a similar amount of flour on the butter. Sprinkle on some grated cheddar, salt and pepper. Repeat the layers. Add milk until it reaches about ¾ the depth of the potato mixture. Cook at 350 degrees for about an hour or until potatoes can be penetrated easily with a fork.

I have been cooking these potatoes since my early married days. I learned a bit of cooking science once when I made these for a backyard party. I had cleverly combined the potatoes and onions well before guests arrived, having been steeped, at that point, in the cleverness of make-ahead recipes. Unfortunately I had not added the milk. To my horror, just as I was about to pop the dish into the oven, I noticed that the potatoes had all turned black! Happily, I was able to quickly recover by slicing more potatoes and onions. But if you are going to make the dish to be cooked at the last minute, cover all the potatoes with milk.

These days, however, I would probably cook the potatoes before the guests come and serve them barely warm or at room temperature. I'm really into room temperature!

Veggies and Side Dishes **79**

Puréed Cauliflower

Here's a lovely alternative to mashed potatoes. You can make adjustments to make it less caloric if you like, but I urge you to try it once with the full strength ingredients. If you don't overcook it, it is delicate and addictively satisfying. This bears no relation to the foul smelling, waterlogged florets we're sometimes served to log up our nine-a-day veggie quota. It has a subtle sweetness and no hint of that cabbage family sulphur-y taste and smell. And you don't have to peel cauliflower! I use an inexpensive, collapsible steamer basket for cooking.

1 Large Head Cauliflower, broken into florets

¾ Cup Half and Half (or milk)

½ Teaspoon Salt

Pepper

1 Tablespoon Butter

Place cauliflower florets over boiling water in a pot equipped with a steamer basket. Meanwhile, heat half and half, ½ teaspoon salt, several grinds of pepper and butter together until butter melts.

Begin testing cauliflower about six minutes after water has come to a boil. When a fork can just penetrate the florets, remove from heat. Pour water from pan and remove steamer basket, placing florets back in the pan. Add about half the hot liquid mixture and purée. I have a hand-held blender which makes this easy, but you may also accomplish the purée by moving the cauliflower to a processor and pulsing and adding as much of the hot cream or milk as you need to reach a mashed potato consistency. Add salt and pepper to taste.

Serves 6.

Brown Rice

Are you choosing brown rice instead of white these days? We are. Do you have as much trouble cooking brown rice as I do? The formula on the back of the package is not remotely related to what works either in amount of cooking liquid or in cooking time. By the time the cooking liquid (double the amount for white rice) has been absorbed, the rice is still underdone and begins to scorch. I have a good pan with permanent marks of a failed batch.

As with other knotty cooking problems, I turned to Cook's Illustrated's *test kitchen for a formula that works. I was relieved to see that they recognized that cooking brown rice is totally different from cooking white rice. Their recipe arrived at satisfyingly chewy, perfectly cooked rice. Delicious enough to be served by itself or as the underpinnings for gravy or meat dishes.*

1 Cup Raw Brown Rice

1 ¾ Cups Water (or Broth or a mixture of the two)

½ Teaspoon Salt, more or less to taste

The secret is cooking the rice *tightly* covered in a 350-degree oven for 50 minutes. Remove from oven but don't lift lid for another 10–15 minutes.

Yields 3 Cups.

We partner with local Master Gardeners to maintain a public "Compost Education Center" in the Cemetery.

Veggies and Side Dishes **81**

Weekday Grits

Food to Die For *has a great recipe for cheese grits to make ahead for a party. The recipe that follows is a weeknight dish. A non-recipe. It's a lovely foil for sausage. Or add some peeled shrimp cooked with a few chopped onions which have been sautéed in butter before adding the shrimp, and you've got Shrimp and Grits. I'll give you the proportions of liquids I use, but I felt free to tamper with the proportions recommended on the grits package and I hope you will too.*

I use Bob's Red Mill "Corn Grits also known as Polenta." I can buy that at my local Kroger. If polenta has missed your market, go ahead and use Quaker Grits. I am currently trying this recipe out on grits bought in bulk.

2 Cups Chicken Broth
½ Cup Water
½ Teaspoon Salt
1 Cup Grits
½ Tablespoon Butter
½ Cup Milk
½ Cup (or to taste) Grated Cheddar

Bring broth, water and salt to a boil over medium heat. Stir in grits and reduce heat to low. Simmer for five to ten minutes until grits have thickened, stirring frequently with a wooden spoon. Add butter. Add milk (more or less than the half cup) to arrive at the consistency you desire. Throw in the cheese and stir until melted.

Serves 2-3.

Writing the Overdue—Way Overdue— Thank You

Unfortunately, I have had too much experience in the Overdue Thank You realm. It embarrasses me to confess that there is frequently too long a lapse 'twixt gift and thank you. My friends know it. Happily they are still my friends.

I have some thoughts on the subject of tardy thank yous. We all know the best and easiest thank you is the result of the reflexive gratitude felt immediately after receipt of a gift. Writing promptly is the best policy. You can accomplish an appreciative declaration in a very few sentences. Superlatives seem natural. Brevity amplifies your gratitude because you need to respond immediately to express your overwhelming appreciation. There is no such thing (in spite of what we learned from E.B. White) as too many exclamation marks in this express thank you. But, that same note written days, or weeks later, seems flip. You can't get away with it. Move to Plan B.

Writing promptly is not always possible, even if the thank you muse is poised for action. One can't always get words on paper right away. Regrettably, if you've delayed writing the note you're going to have to write a more thorough—and much longer—note. A letter. If you've received a book, you're going to have to write a book report. If you've received wine, you've got to remember whether you were given Cabernet or Prosecco. And what you paired it with!

Here are some tips when writing your Overdue Thank You. Briefly express your apology for tardiness. Do not grovel. Do not make excuses, unless you truly have been in a coma from which you have just awakened. Do not spend more than one sentence apologizing. Here's where you might consider how you feel and try to express that feeling. That soul search has given me these openers: "I wish it had not taken me so long to let you know how much I like the lawn mower sharpener." Or "It has taken me much longer than I would have liked to let you know…"

And here are some other suggestions from friends about dealing with tardiness:

"Mercy! It's taken me so long to say 'Merci'!"

"I hope the statute of limitations has not run out."

"I have enjoyed the marvelous lawn mower sharpener many times and just wish I could have gotten my gratitude on paper before now...."

You can probably arrive at your own sincere solution to the tardy problem by thinking, "What do I want to convey here?" and then write that down, in words that are natural to you. But remember. Don't belabor the apology!

We got a wedding thank you from a young person I like a lot. It began, "I can't believe it's been eighteen months since we got married..." and then proceeded to a very winning thank you. I was delighted to see a kindred spirit in tardiness with a good solution for discharging guilt in the first sentence.

Whatever and whenever you write should be done with connecting warmth and sincerity. This should apply to your condolence notes and congratulatory notes as well as to your thank you notes. A very formulaic thank you, even if sent immediately but without the flavor of spontaneity and enthusiasm, can be disappointing to receive. Oddly, I feel checked off the recipient's to-do list. I expect some warmth and gratitude however it is achieved. This is probably unreasonable of me. Better to acknowledge the gift right away in any form. I guess . . .

Here's a tip to anybody who might owe me a thank you. I probably don't remember whether I've gotten one or not. And something else, I won't remember it unless it's very, very good or very, very bad. Some thank yous ought not to be written.

One last thing on the subject of the tardy thank you: Gena Davidson, who is a prompt writer of the very best thank you notes says, "It's NEVER too late to write a thank you."

The Cemetery's Lotus Pond and Butterfly Garden are teeming with life. Students love searching for orange goldfish in the pond.

Katie Sneary and Stephen Levesque departed for married life at the Station House Museum on April 25, 2003.

Salads

Baby Greens, Pear, Walnut and Blue Cheese Salad

Just to assure you I'm totally with it, I now present a salad I pulled from the internet. It's my favorite side-dish salad. Somewhere I had enjoyed a green salad with pears, blue cheese and walnuts, and I wanted to find the dressing, so I Googled the salad. Voila! There was the very salad I sought with a lemon-olive oil-shallot dressing. This came from the Hot and Hot Fish Club in Birmingham, Alabama. I'm so glad they shared it with Google and me! We eat this salad as long in the fall as Harry and David can keep us supplied with perfectly ripened Maverick Royal Riviera pears. Once deprived of those, I have to abandon the salad. Hope springs eternal, and I try to buy pears in the supermarket, but they never seem to achieve ripeness. Pears advance from hard-as-a-brick (in which state they remain for two weeks) to overripe and mushy. They're perfectly ripe for 6 minutes in the middle of one night!

Dressing

3 Tablespoons Fresh Lemon Juice

1 Tablespoon Dijon Mustard

1 Medium Shallot, minced

1 ½ Teaspoons Chopped Fresh Thyme

½ Cup Olive Oil

Salt and Pepper, to taste

1 5-Ounce Bag Mixed Baby Greens

2 Large Ripe Pears, halved, cored, thinly sliced lengthwise

1 Cup Crumbled Blue Cheese

1 Cup Walnuts, toasted and coarsely chopped

Whisk first 4 ingredients in a small bowl to blend. Gradually whisk in oil. Season with salt and pepper to taste.

Toss greens in a salad bowl with enough dressing to coat lightly. Divide greens among 6 plates. Top with pear slices, dividing equally. Sprinkle with cheese and walnuts. Drizzle lightly with remaining dressing and serve.

Serves 6.

I have found that I can double the dressing recipe and enjoy several nights of salads.

Nina Pillsbury's Black Bean and Corn Salad

This salad came by way of Linn Ong, who has supplied me with some of my very favorite and most-used recipes. Here's another delicious salad that can be made ahead—always an advantage in a salad. Linn credits Nina Pillsbury with this recipe.

1 Can Black Beans, rinsed and drained

1 Can Sweet Corn

½ Cup Orange or Yellow Pepper, chopped

¼ Cup Green Onion, chopped

½ Cup Fresh Cilantro, chopped

One Tomato, cut into chunks

Juice of ½ Lime

¼ Cup Mild Taco Sauce

Salt and Pepper, to taste

Kernels from one or more ears of fresh corn (optional)

Combine all ingredients in a large bowl. Make a day ahead. Keeps three days or so.

Serves 15.

P. S. Linn says she cheated by making this the same day served and that it was fine.

Taco Bean Salad

This recipe is from Harriet Hellewell, who contributed the popular Pull Apart Coffee Cake in Food to Die For. *She called me with another favorite that she has made many times since the seventies when it was referred to as "Frito Salad." It has been her most frequent contribution to potlucks for 40 years. She uses Kraft Catalina dressing. In the seventies she decanted it into another jar to imply "homemade." She confesses, but has long since given up that bother since friends love the salad too much to give a whit about the source of the dressing.*

You'll notice that this recipe calls for a large proportion of tomatoes. Harriet says that this is a great midsummer recipe to absorb an overflow from the garden

5 Tomatoes, chopped into walnut-sized pieces

2 Green Peppers, chopped into walnut-sized pieces

1 Large Onion, chopped

2 Cans Kidney Beans (Harriet uses light but says it doesn't matter), drained

8 Ounces Cheddar Cheese, grated

1 Small Jar Kraft Catalina Dressing

1 Medium Bag Fritos, broken up a bit but not pulverized

First four ingredients can be combined ahead of time. The last three ingredients should be added just before serving. This salad doesn't keep. The Doritos become soggy and unappealing.

Serves 12

Composting

Our kitchen doesn't have a garbage disposal. Even while acknowledging, in the big scheme, this is a minor deprivation, I used to feel sorry for myself. It was sometimes necessary to freeze odoriferous remains until garbage pickup day. Actually, the only really troublesome time came at Thanksgiving when, years ago, we entertained the greater Ward family. Every year, before you could warn them off, helpful people would scrape bits of dressing and turkey and peas into my non-existent disposal. The first job of cleanup was always unplugging the kitchen sink.

One day, hoping for sympathy, I mentioned to Sandra Carrington that I had no disposal. She said she didn't either! And Annie Massie who was nearby, said she didn't either. They began to extol the wonders of composting. If they could do it, so could I. So I sent away to The Garden Supply Company for modestly priced wire bins. I have three (they attach to each other) for compost in different stages of ripening.

Well, now I think I prefer growing compost to flowers. I'm not a compost turner, and I don't think too much about what I layer. It may take a little longer not to shuffle and not to layer leaves, soil, peelings in some sort of casserole order, but in a couple of years everything (excepting peach pits) turns into the richest soil.

Some people admire their specimen peonies. I rush out to see how much the leaves added on Monday have sunk by Thursday. Added over a few weeks, one compost pile can absorb all the leaves from one large cherry tree. The tree, I'll admit, is very cooperative, compost-wise. It drops leaves starting mid-summer and continues shedding for the next two months. All the while, I'm adding peach peelings, onion skins, cantaloupe rinds, outer leaves of romaine, lemon rinds, and so on between every delivery of leaves.

This is recycling at it best! I admire all the little bugs and bacteria that are busy, busy, busy making rich soil from my discards. Rather than feeling guilty about hungry people who did not have benefit of the squash I didn't get to in time, I can feel virtuous. Well, sort of.

In case you are wondering whether my compost pile attracts vermin, the answer is no. At least not that I know of. A host of little bugs, fliers and crawlers, react with great activity when I add a bucket of kitchen waste, but since they, along with some healthy bacteria, are responsible for turning my grapefruit into rich soil, I can only be grateful to them.

I never add any cooked foods. I never add any kind of fat or grease to the pile. Apparently that's what begins to attract you-know-whats.

I invite you to come view my compost. It's beautiful and is in full bloom summer and winter.

Old City Cemetery from above, taken on Rose Festival Day, 2006
Photo by Nancy Blackwell Marion

Bread and Breakfast

Raised Waffles

For years I used my grandmother's recipe for Cream Waffles. Actually I cooked her Cream Waffles in her double-sided waffle iron until it gave up the ghost after 60 years of service. In spite of many efforts to have it revived, I finally had to declare it dead. Nevertheless it is still on the shelf in my basement…

I got a new All-Clad waffle iron, and though I miss the double-sided contraption, this one is non-stick and cooks the waffles beautifully. When I used my grandmother's iron, I always had to throw away the first waffle, which was used to prime the iron's surface!

About the time I got the new waffle iron, I bought Marion Cunningham's book, Lost Recipes. *I always buy her wonderful books. You'll remember that she has edited the more recent Fannie Farmer cookbooks.*

She has THE most wonderful recipe for waffles there you'll ever taste. I checked, and there the recipe has been all those years in my old Fannie Farmer (the gold one) and I'd been missing it for 45 years! Here it is.

½ Cup Warm Water
1 Package Active Dry Yeast
2 Cups Milk, warmed
½ Cup (1 Stick) Butter, melted
1 Teaspoon Salt
1 Teaspoon Sugar
2 Cups All-Purpose Flour
2 Eggs
¼ Teaspoon Baking Soda

Use a mixing bowl large enough to accommodate ingredients doubling in size. Put warm water in the bowl and sprinkle in yeast. After a few minutes, when yeast is dissolved, add milk, melted butter, salt, sugar and flour. Beat until smooth with a hand mixer or whisk. Cover the bowl with plastic wrap and let stand overnight at room temperature.

Just before baking the waffles, mix in the eggs and baking soda and whisk until thoroughly combined. You will think the batter is too thin. It's not. Pour into waffle iron and bake.

This recipe fills my large square waffle iron 4 times. If you have an old waffle iron (Sigh!), it will make 8 waffles.

P. S. I once mistakenly added the eggs and baking soda the night before and the waffles were still wonderful. I did add an additional half-teaspoon of baking soda when I discovered my error.

Scrambled Omelet

This is a solo treat for breakfast or supper. I'm usually inspired to make this when I have a little pico de gallo or salsa in the fridge. I generally have a little yogurt and grated cheese too. It's good enough to double and share with a mate. Just make sure it's not someone who's too into classic omelets.

Butter
1 Egg
½ Teaspoon Water
1 Tablespoon Yogurt
Pinch Salt
Grind of Pepper
1 Heaping Tablespoons Pico de Gallo
Grated Cheese

Lightly beat egg, water, yogurt, salt and pepper. Pour into a buttered omelet pan that has been heated over medium heat until the butter has just begun to sizzle. After the egg mixture has begun to firm, add the pico and the cheese and stir to scramble the omelet. Cook until as firm as you desire.

Bet you have your own version of eggs. I'd like to hear about it.

Judy's Bran Muffins

Judy Schulz brought these Bran Muffins on a beach trip. They're delicious as well as healthy. She made them even healthier by halving the sugar in the recipe as it was given to her. The batter is ready for fresh muffins in any quantity when you need it.

1 15-Ounce Box Raisin Bran Cereal

1 ½ Cups Sugar

5 Cups All-Purpose Flour

5 Teaspoons Baking Soda

2 Teaspoons Salt

1 Quart Buttermilk

1 Cup Oil (Safflower or Canola)

2 Eggs

Mix dry ingredients. Add buttermilk, oil and eggs. Mix well. You will think that it doesn't look quite mixed, but it is!

The mixture will thicken as it stands. Store in a large glass or crockery container in the refrigerator for as long as six weeks.

To bake:

Preheat oven to 400 degrees. Without stirring batter, spoon the portion you want into greased muffin tins—for just the number of muffins you want. Bake for about 15 minutes.

Makes 5 Dozen Muffins.

Bread and Breakfast **95**

Super Pancake

Mina Wood has sent this recipe by email with a note: "This is fun and great for a bunch of children. We made it a lot of times at Pawleys Island and it comes out like a giant popover."

1 Stick Butter
1 Cup Milk
2 Large Eggs
1 Cup Flour

Toppings:
Juice from 1 Lemon
Powdered Sugar

Preheat oven to 450 degrees. Put butter in black iron skillet and place in oven. While butter is melting, in a bowl combine milk, eggs, flour and mix quickly until just blended. Pour into sizzling butter in skillet and pop back into oven. After 10 minutes, turn down to 350 degrees and leave for 15 minutes. Take out and squeeze juice from 1 lemon over pancake and sprinkle powdered sugar over it. Cut into slices.

Serves 1–6

State senator and World War I veteran A. D. Barksdale delivered the address at the unveiling of the new Veterans Bench in the Confederate Section on Memorial Day, 1931.

Courtesy of Polly Garbee

Hot Water Cornbread

Try this recipe at your own risk. Hot Water Cornbread, like black-eyed peas, is probably an acquired taste. I have been casting around trying to recreate what my brother and I remember as favorite foods when we were growing up. Hot Water Cornbread was high on the list. Unfortunately I didn't pay quite enough attention to how it was made. This is almost it.

In summer, hot water cornbread was often served with meatless menus consisting of high summer vegetables such as purple hull peas, okra, tomatoes and squash. In winter it was frequently served with split pea soup. It is hearty, with a crusty outside, a moist inside and is delicious with a meatless meal.

Many recipes for hot water cornbread call for frying, but at our house the "pones" were baked.

2 Cups White Unbleached Cornmeal

2 Tablespoons Vegetable Oil or Bacon Drippings

¼ Teaspoon Baking Soda

½ Teaspoon Salt

½ Teaspoon Sugar

1 ½ Cups Boiling Water (although you will probably use less)

Preheat oven to 475 degrees. Combine cornmeal, oil, baking soda, salt and sugar. Add boiling water until you arrive at a consistency that can be patted together into flat pones, approximately 2 inches long and 1 ½ inches wide. Place an inch apart on a greased baking sheet and bake on upper rack in oven for about 25 minutes or until light brown. Serve with butter.

Makes 15–16.

Housekeeping Tips from a Person with Dubious Housekeeping Credentials

- Make your bed as soon as you crawl out of it. All occupants of that bed should help with the bed making. Making your bed goes as far as any single gesture can to bring calm to a day. Even if the bed is surrounded by chaos, the flat, smooth surface offers instant serenity and order. Besides, it's a good place to put stuff. Having a partner help with bed making means the job takes less than half as long. It establishes early in the day a just division of labor.

  My husband, Peter, brought the good bed-making practice to our marriage. I was definitely of the Why-would-you-want-to-go-to-that-trouble-when-you're-going-to-undo-it-all-so-soon school. Peter's father had instilled bed-making imperative in him back when he was in elementary school by offering Peter $10.00 if he would make his bed for a week. Since ten dollars was ten dollars in the fifties, Peter performed with admirable proficiency and the reward was paid. Then Colonel Ward said "I see that you know how to make your bed. Now do it for the rest of your life." And he has. And I help.

- When your gas tank reaches the ¼ mark, fill it as soon as you can comfortably do so. That allows you to fill it on your schedule. Waiting until it's almost empty means you have to abide by the tank's schedule! A tank is not very understanding about appointments to be kept. An empty tank can create a minor crisis.

  Should you miss that flight because of the unfilled tank, though, here is an exercise to console you while you wait for the next flight. You can calculate how many fewer times you'll have to fill your tank in your lifetime if you wait until the tank is down to the last drop before you fill it up.

  Bulletin—Just In!! I've heard that the Car Guys say it's better for the car to keep the tank at least half filled. I won't investigate further, just in case I misheard this bit of support for my advice!

- Take Wineaway (a product to spray on immediately after wine has been spilled to avoid a stain), rather than wine as a hostess present. Or take a small, really good bottle of olive oil.

- Let the table gear you already have be your guide as to party menus. Better yet, pull something out of hiding that belonged to your mother or grandmother and think of a way to use it—even if it's not for its original assignment. Using what you own will bring nostalgic pleasures. And it's thrifty! Pull out the fondue pot. Give the prissy parfait glasses a bath. Layer something unconventional in a trifle bowl. Exercise your party linens. Have a party using things you've never used.

- Here's something I started doing several years ago that has made it easier to retrieve sets of things (such as demitasse cups and saucers) from a cabinet. Buy a metal basket coated with vinyl and stash your sets of things that are apt to be needed all at once in it. My basket is about 12 inches by 8 inches, and about 4 ½ inches high. It has drop handles and I think I bought it at the Container Store. At any rate, your demitasse cups are probably not stored on the easiest-to-get-to shelf and getting them out is usually a precarious act. The basket allows you to remove the stacked and nested pieces from the shelf with ease and safety. Sometimes I take the cups and saucers to the table in the basket (it's inoffensively white).

I have another basket that's filled with a dozen or so assorted small vases. In the basket, the small vases don't get lost behind bigger ones and it's easier to see the choices if the whole collection is out at once. The unused vases can go right back to their higher shelf with minimal effort.

Guests in the Kitchen

Here are some thoughts on helping your host/hostess.

When I am a guest, I am truly happy to help the host or hostess in the kitchen. However, I want to be given a specific job. Some people seem to intuit what jobs will be most helpful, but I, in spite of years in the kitchen, am not one of those people. I need to have someone say, "Slice the bread and here's the bread knife." Or "Fill the water glasses and here's the pitcher."

I also heed "Keep your seat," since I do not like to have half the guests pop up from the table to help me when it's my turn to be hostess. It just confuses me. I read with puzzlement—and no particular admiration—about famous hostesses who invite everybody into the kitchen to share the preparation. Does that really happen?

The other thing is that when people leap to their feet to help clear the table between courses, conversation disintegrates. Do your part for the party. Stay put.

I am easily distracted, so maybe that has something to do with my feeling that "Many hands make chaos."

I'm afraid I am also very particular about how I want things to be done. I know I should get over that, but that's my problem. My guests should sit back and enjoy it.

Which brings me to another kitchen issue. I don't want help with cleanup either. I would much prefer to pretend it doesn't have to happen. I have never felt compelled to leave the kitchen spotless before I go to bed. In fact, the only cleanup I do immediately after a party is to refrigerate food and start the dishwasher. I am probably in bed before most of my guests!

Next morning I get a sort of zen pleasure doing the dishes. I've enjoyed using my "things," and cleaning up when I'm rested and not rushed is a curious luxury.

So trust me when I say, "Please don't get up."

Winterberry frames the Chapel during the 2012 Wreaths Across America ceremony.

Lotus blooms in the Cemetery pond are a striking sight every summer.

Desserts

Blackberry Cobbler

From the time the first blueberries, blackberries and raspberries show up in our farmers' market, I begin to make cobblers for Saturday morning breakfasts. An hour and a half after Peter and I are home from the market we're enjoying a very fresh, very hot, berry cobbler. We have a bit of a good cheddar cheese alongside.

Here's the cobbler that's very much like the one I grew up with. The berries are cooked in pie crust. Sometimes loose pieces of pie crust are buried in the berries and appear in the cooked cobbler as berry-saturated dumplings. Yum!

Feel free to use other berries with or instead of the blackberries.

Pastry

1 ¼ Cups Flour

¼ Cup Cold Butter

½ Teaspoon Salt

2 to 3 Tablespoons Iced Water

Filling

3 to 4 Cups Blackberries (or other berries or a mixture)

1 ½ Teaspoons Vanilla

½ Cup to 1 Cup Sugar—depending on sweetness of the berries

3 Tablespoons Flour

¼ Teaspoon Salt

2 Tablespoons Butter

A Little Lemon Juice—only if the berries aren't very tart and flavorful

Place butter, flour and salt in processor container. Pulse processor on and off briefly to mix and to break butter into small pieces. Add 2 tablespoons iced water and process until a cohesive dough forms. If it doesn't begin to form a ball in about 30 seconds, add water by teaspoons until it does.

For easier rolling, chill dough for half an hour. Place the dough between two sheets of parchment paper and roll out to a shape large enough so the dough drapes over the sides of the baking dish you choose. Don't worry about neat. Ragged edges are a must!

Preheat oven to 450 degrees. Line a baking dish (1 ½ quart round Pyrex is fine) with pastry. Place half the berries in the pastry. Add ½ to 1 Cup sugar, depending on sweetness of the berries and your taste. Sprinkle flour and salt on top. Add butter in thin slices. Add remainder of berries. Draw surplus pastry (which has been draped over the sides of the dish) over the berry mixture. Don't worry if it doesn't fully cover. In fact, don't worry about anything! It will be delicious!

Bake at 450 degrees for 10 minutes and then reduce heat to 350 degrees and bake for another 40 to 50 minutes until pastry is delicately brown.

Serves 4–6.

Caketop Blackberry Cobbler

We have a cobbler fest midsummer every year when the blackberries come in at the farmers' market. Although this is not what I think of when I think of a cobbler, it is an alternative to piecrust-y cobblers. This is one of those magic recipes. Place blackberries on top of batter and lo and behold, an hour in the oven and the fruit and batter have exchanged places! The berries are buried under a luscious moist cake.

6 Tablespoons Butter

¾ Cup Flour

1 Cup Sugar

2 Teaspoons Baking Powder

½ Teaspoon Salt

¾ Cup Milk

2 Cups Blackberries

Additional ½ Cup Sugar (more if your berries are not very sweet)

Melt butter in an 8" square pan. Sift together flour, 1 cup sugar, baking powder and salt. Mix dry ingredients with milk. Pour into pan of melted butter and do not mix. Mix together blackberries and ½ cup sugar. Pour fruit over batter, but do not stir. Bake for approximately 1 hour.

Serves 6.

Strawberry Shortcake a la Prescott

When strawberry season came to Prescott, Arkansas, we made the most of it. There were no berries from California to delude you into thinking the season lasted more than three or four weeks. Even allowing for enhancement by 71-year-old memory, strawberry shortcake, as known in Prescott, was divine. This is far superior to those soggy spongecake cups or ordinary biscuits usually enlisted for shortcake duty. By the way, why do they call those little cakes sold in supermarkets shortcake shells? Nothing short about them. Please note that those Southwest Arkansas cooks were way ahead of New York chefs in "stacking."

Strawberries

Sugar

Whipping Cream, whipped until not quite stiff

Shortcake Crust, tender enough to be good, sturdy enough to support the stack

Shortcake Crust

1 Cup Flour

6 Tablespoons Shortening

¼ Teaspoon Salt

2 Tablespoons Ice Water

Place flour, shortening and salt in processor. Blend with pulses. Add enough of the water to form into dough. Roll pie crust thin. Cut into three inch circles (or squares if you don't have a cutter that big). Bake in a 400-degree oven for 10 to 15 minutes until lightly browned.

Shortcake Assembly

Add a little sugar to the strawberries 10 or 15 minutes before serving. This will render a little juice from the berries. Sugaring them very long in advance will make the berries a soggy mess, so don't be tempted to get ahead!

Place a piecrust round on a dessert plate. Place a few berries on the pastry. Top the berries with a second piecrust round. Add more berries. Pour cream, whipped just enough to ooze luxuriantly down the sides, over all.

Wistar Nelligan's Apple Pie

Our good friend Wistar makes a classic apple pie. He uses two pie shells from the freezer case. One of them serves as the upper crust.

5 Cups Golden Delicious Apples, peeled and sliced thin

2 Tablespoons Flour

½ Cup White Sugar

¼ Cup Dark Brown Sugar

¼ Teaspoon Salt

⅛ Teaspoon Nutmeg, preferably freshly grated (or more to taste)

⅛ Teaspoon Allspice

Rind of One Lemon, grated

Pinch of Ginger

Two Frozen Pie Crusts

Mix all ingredients in a large bowl.

Place the mixture in bottom crust, cover with your choice of top crust and bake for 15 minutes at 450 degrees. Reduce heat to 350 degrees and bake for another 20 to 35 minutes until nicely browned.

Serve with ice cream or a good cheddar cheese.

Serves 6-8.

Almond Macaroons

Maybe you thought that macaroons were unachieveable by ordinary mortals. Not so! To my surprise, I found that they don't require a degree in pastry. In Julia Childs & More Company, *nestled in amongst the explanations of how to prepare lobster soufflé for a luncheon, is this simplest and easiest of cookie recipes for the most irresistible of cookies. Approximately the same directions, minus the almond extract, can be found on the label of a can of Solo Almond Paste. I've been making them without the almond extract.*

8 Ounces Almond Paste

1 Cup Sugar

¼ Teaspoon Salt

⅜ Cup Egg Whites (that's usually a little less than two large egg whites)

¼ Teaspoon Almond Extract (optional)

Preheat oven to 325 degrees. Line two cookie sheets with parchment paper or with brown paper bags, cut to fit. Paper grocery bags may be used, but avoid those with print.

Process almond paste with on and off spurts in a food processor until the almond paste resembles brown sugar. Add sugar and process. Add salt, egg whites and almond extract. Mix until smooth. Drop by ¾" blobs onto parchment paper. Flatten using a spoon dipped in water. Bake for 20–25 minutes until macaroons are lightly browned and crusty on top. Let dry for an hour or so—if you can wait! Store (but not for long) in an airtight container. Makes two dozen.

P. S. There are good recipes for macaroons that have gone a bit stale. Try my grandmother's easy Macaroon Bisque Ice Cream or Macaroon Custard in this book.

Desserts **107**

You-Can't-Stop-Eating-Them Cookies

Several years ago, Jane White and I made a trip to Thomson, Georgia, on a cookbook promotion trip. Marsha Hughes, a delightful person, had come upon Food to Die For *by way of the Tabasco prize, and connected that with her involvement in launching a city museum in Thomson. Jane and I were treated royally and I think often of our good time there.*

While we were there, we were treated to You-Can't-Stop-Eating-Them Cookies made by Bob Gibson, who generously shared his recipe. Back in Lynchburg, Jane White and I make them frequently. And, by the way, you can't—stop eating them, that is.

1 Cup Butter, softened
1 Cup Sugar
1 ½ Cups All-Purpose Flour
½ Teaspoon Salt
½ Teaspoon Baking Powder
½ Teaspoon Baking Soda
1 Teaspoon Vanilla
2 Cups Rice Crispies Cereal
½ Cup Pecans, chopped

Preheat oven to 350 degrees. Cream butter and sugar together with an electric mixer. Combine flour, salt, baking powder and baking soda and add to butter/sugar mixture and continue to beat until thoroughly combined. Add vanilla. Stir in Rice Crispies and pecans.

Drop dough by the teaspoonful onto a greased cookie sheet. Flatten each cookie with a fork. Bake cookies about 10 minutes, but only until they have begun to turn brown at the edge. Cool on a wire rack.

Thank you, Bobby, who made these delicious cookies for us to try.

Mary's Chocolate Cake

Dee Doyle, expert proof reader, is also a great cook. When I asked for a recipe from her, this is what she gave me. It's easy, delicious, requires no frosting and serves many. A one-bowl cake! Her friend, Mary Hulick, gave her the recipe for what Mary's family calls Picnic Cake.

2 Cups Flour

2 Cups Sugar

1 Teaspoon Baking Soda

1 Teaspoon Salt

½ Teaspoon Baking Powder

¾ Cup Buttermilk

½ Cup Shortening

2 Eggs

1 Teaspoon Vanilla

4 Ounces Unsweetened Chocolate, melted

Powdered sugar, for dusting on top

Preheat oven to 350 degrees. Measure all ingredients except powdered sugar into a large mixer bowl. Mix at low speed for ½ minute, then beat at high speed for 3 minutes.

Pour into greased 9" x 13" pan. Bake at 350 degrees for 30 minutes.

Dust with powdered sugar when the cake has cooled and you're ready to serve.

Dee adds that if you get yourself one of those 9" x 13" pans with a lid, you, too, are ready for a picnic!

Joan Roberson's Delicious and Easy Brownies

1 Stick Butter
2 Ounces Unsweetened Chocolate
2 Eggs
1 Cup Sugar
½ Cup Flour
¼ Teaspoon Salt
1 Teaspoon Vanilla
⅔ Cup Toasted Pecan Pieces

Melt together over low heat the butter and chocolate.

Stir together the eggs and sugar.

Stir together chocolate mixture and egg mixture and add the remaining ingredients.

Pour into greased 8" square pan and bake at 350 for approximately 20 minutes.

Many people wear period attire to the annual Confederate Memorial Day Service at Old City Cemetery.

Mimi's Chocolate Fudge Pie

My cousin, Mary Carleton Young, has shared her grandmother's recipe. She says it is elegant, rich and quick when you have surprise guests. Actually, it's lovely to have an elegant, rich and quick recipe even when your guests are not surprises! I am happy to pass along this divine crustless pie. This recipe is going to make you happy you bought this book!

1 Stick Butter
2 Squares Unsweetened Chocolate
4 Eggs
1 ¼ Cups Sugar
1 Tablespoon Flour
1 Teaspoon Vanilla
Pinch of Salt

Melt butter and chocolate together. Beat eggs with sugar, flour, vanilla and salt and fold in the chocolate and butter. Pour into an ungreased small pie plate and place in a larger pie plate half filled with cold water. Place in a cold oven and turn oven to 300 degrees. Bake for one hour. Cool. Cut into small slices and serve with whipped cream, fresh raspberries (or strawberries) and a sprig of mint, if you have it. Ice cream works well too.

Note: Mary Carleton says this is a very old family recipe when pie plates of varying sizes were easy to find. I usually place the water in a nine inch or larger pie plate so a six to eight inch plate would be best for the pie itself.

Serves 8.

Desserts **111**

Chocolate Brittle

Here's a recipe that travels like wildfire. Everybody who tastes Chocolate Brittle wants the recipe. It has such curious ingredients. It's cousin to a recipe that has circulated for years using graham crackers. This one uses saltines! And it's better! I had it first when I was a visitor at a meeting of the Hillside Garden Club at Laura Rosser's. She generously gave the recipe to me and to every other person at the meeting who didn't already have it.

Saltine Crackers
2 Sticks Butter
1 Cup Brown Sugar
2 Cups Chocolate Chips
1 ½ Cups Chopped Pecans

Line a rimmed cookie sheet (I use a 17"x 11" sheet) with aluminum foil. Spray foil with Pam. Place saltines (salted side up) on foil in a single layer to fill pan.

Put the butter and sugar in a saucepan and bring to a boil.

Pour hot butter and brown sugar mixture over crackers and bake at 350 degrees for 15 to 20 minutes. Make sure crackers have not bunched at one end of the pan. Remove from oven and sprinkle with 2 cups of Chocolate Chips. Spread softened chips with spatula. Sprinkle with chopped Pecans. Freeze uncovered on cookie sheet for 24 hours. Break into pieces (which need not be in squares). Store in airtight container.

Make this when you have lots of people to feed, or you will probably eat it all yourself and die!

Chocolate Sauce

Those of you familiar with Food to Die For *may recognize this recipe. I include it here with a couple of changes. Our grandson, Tucker, wanted to make sure I didn't leave out this improved version from his mother, Lisa.*

The main change (Lisa's) is that the evaporated milk, called for in the first recipe, has been traded in for the real thing: whipping cream.

The other change is that I have reduced the sugar by half a cup. Peter likes a blast of chocolate. He would probably like it even better if I reduced the sugar by another half cup. You can suit yourself.

½ Cup (1 Stick) Butter
4 Squares Unsweetened Chocolate
2 ½ Cups Sugar
¼ Teaspoon Salt
12 Ounces Whipping Cream
2 Teaspoons Vanilla

Melt butter and chocolate in top of double boiler. Add sugar and salt. Add cream.

Stir until smooth and thick. Stir in vanilla. Especially good served warm.

Desserts **113**

Macaroon Bisque Ice Cream

Here's a divine concoction my grandmother used to serve. Oddly, it's hard to identify the sherry as an ingredient, but the combination of flavors is scrumptious. This is a great way to use macaroons that have gone a bit stale. It's good enough so that you may want to make macaroons just for this. Bet your grandmother served this too.

1 Quart Vanilla Ice Cream

8 to 12 Small to Medium Macaroons (don't get too concerned about quantity)

½ Cup Cream Sherry

Remove ice cream from freezer to soften for about 20 minutes. About the length of time it takes you to get home from Kroger is right! Break macaroons into a mixer bowl. Pour sherry over and then turn on mixer to hasten breakdown of macaroons into small pieces. Suit yourself as to how small. Add ice cream and mix for about a minute at slow speed until ingredients are blended.

Serves 6, though your guests will wish they had more.

P. S. This works with other stale cookies too.

Macaroon Custard

This is a delicious make-ahead dessert ideal for a crowd since the recipe can be easily doubled. It can be served in bistro glasses, compotes, or even in small plastic wine glasses in a pinch.

I used to make this for large Thanksgiving gatherings. I could make it a couple of days ahead, put it in the serving glasses, cover and slide it on a tray into the refrigerator. Only a whipped cream dollop to be added at the last minute!

2 Cups Milk, scalded

2 Whole Eggs (or 4 Yolks)

⅛ Teaspoon Salt

4 Tablespoons Sugar

1 ½ Dozen Macaroons (more or less depending on size of macaroon)

1 Tablespoon Plain Gelatin, softened in 2 tablespoons cold water

1 Tablespoon Almond Extract

1 Pint Heavy Cream, whipped

Beat together eggs, salt and sugar, then add hot milk to mixture. Crumble macaroons into mixture and cook in top of double-boiler until mixture barely coats spoon (should be very thin). Soften gelatin in cold water; stir into hot mixture until dissolved. Cool. Add almond extract. Fold in whipped cream. Pour into dessert glasses and chill at least 4 hours. Serve topped with additional whipped cream.

Serves 12

Sallie's Chocolate Tarts

Here's a recipe from Sallie Craddock that you don't want to miss. It's another of the great ones from Good Cookin' from the Heart of Virginia *which is no longer in print. Sallie has given me the go-ahead to include it here.*

- ½ Cup (1 Stick) Butter, melted
- 1 Cup Sugar
- 1 Cup Light Brown Sugar
- 2 Eggs, lightly beaten
- 3 Tablespoons Flour
- 3 Tablespoons Cocoa
- ⅓ Cup Milk
- 1 Teaspoon Vanilla
- 12–14 Unbaked Pastry Tart Shells
- Sweetened Whipped Cream for Garnish

Mix first 8 ingredients together and pour into tart shells. Bake in a preheated 350 degree oven for 25 minutes. Cool. Serve with whipped cream.

Assuming your grocery has the small frozen pastry shells (VIP brand, eight to a box) alongside the frozen pie crusts, this recipe couldn't be easier!

Ever since goats first arrived at the Cemetery in March 2004, they have been a constant source of amusement for staff and visitors alike.

Terry Tosh's Fudge

A delightful visitor to the Cemetery several years ago was Terry Tosh. She's a cemetery person through and through. She spends a good bit of time landscaping family plots at the Hollywood Cemetery in Richmond. She's also an active advocate of the overall upkeep of that beautiful and historic cemetery. Jane White and Terry are mutual admirers and I enjoyed joining them for sandwiches at the Station House in the Old City Cemetery.

Terry told me she had a must-have, sure-thing recipe. You'll want to rush right into the kitchen and make this fudge since you probably already have all the ingredients on hand!

4 ½ Cups Sugar

One 12-Ounce Can Evaporated Milk

3 Cups (18 Ounces) Semi-sweet Chocolate Chips

2 Sticks Butter (1 Cup)

3 Tablespoons Vanilla (Yes, that's tablespoons)

Optional (not in Terry's recipe):

Whipping Cream in Place of the Evaporated Milk

2 Cups Walnut Pieces

1 Teaspoon Salt (because I always add salt to anything sweet)

Line a jellyroll pan (10 ½" x 15 ½" x 1") with waxed paper. Into a big pot on stove, dump sugar and evaporated milk (or cream). Stir constantly and bring to low boil for exactly 6 minutes. Remove from heat. Stir in semi-sweet chocolate chips and butter and stir until smooth. Finally add vanilla. Stir until thoroughly blended. Pour into lined jellyroll pan. Spread evenly and the whole surface will become shiny. Cool, then refrigerate 6 hours (bet you cheat) before cutting and packaging and sharing. Keeps 6 weeks. Terry says she keep squares in the crisper drawer for emergencies!

P. S. I recently sent a batch off to grandsons at camp and I got a thank you! So my whole family thanks you, Terry!

Desserts **117**

Favorite Things, Favorite Even When the New Has Worn Off

There are things that seem so important to have. They are the must-haves of every decade that seem to be placed so attractively in friends' homes. They are the apparel essentials that set off the most niftily dressed from the rest of us. They are the with-it cars with foreign profiles. All of us have to admit to noticing these things even if we don't, or are not able to, submit.

When we first married, Peter and I were lucky enough to be furnished from the outset with overflow furniture from our parents. We had a nice Lawson sofa that seemed to be comfortable enough. Nevertheless, I felt absolutely deprived because we didn't have matching end tables topped by matching lamps. I was totally focused on that terrible shortage.

Happily for us, since we never retire any furniture, early poverty saved us from the so-longed-for sofa accessories which would have forever identified us with the year we were married. Probably also a valuable nudge toward maturity, though I can't admit that the lesson cured me of the lust for the trendy!

There are a few possessions, however, that I take pleasure in every single time I use them. Trendy, if they ever were, does not account for my delight. The new does not wear off. There is renewed satisfaction each time they're called upon. I do not find myself wishing for a replacement. You will notice that, in general, they are not costly items. Rather they are generally humble and basic and do their jobs well.

- My black iron skillet.

- My Totes umbrella.

- My white oak baskets from Arkansas—especially the lunch basket I use at the grocery store.

- An Italian necklace my mother gave me. I've worn it for almost 50 years, every day, even in the shower.

- Big sheets of engraved Crane's wedding weight stationery. For when a "just a note'" will not do.

- My Joyce Chen Scissors. Get some immediately. I lost mine in the garden (it's no tidier than my kitchen) several months ago, and after considerable time spent searching, I gave up and went to The Farm Basket, which sells them. Eek! They were out of them! Nothing to do but eat out until they were back in stock! They're needle-nosed and strong. So strong that they can cut a lobster shell. So refined that they can sneak in and cut just a sprig or two of an herb. They have red handles so you can locate them in a disorderly kitchen easily. But not in the garden.

- An iron teapot my friend Marie gave me.

- A one-cup, wren-shaped teapot our son Peter gave me; it nestles appealingly in one's hand. Warms the hand and the heart.

- My black canvas Keds. They're hard to find for some reason. The black canvas Keds now have a white sole that shrieks you've got on your comfy Keds. ALL-Black Keds are great travel shoes. They make leather and nubuck all-black Keds, but it's not the same. I finally went online and found them at Keds.com (surprise, surprise) and ordered a lifetime supply. Remember, I'm over 70.

- McCann's Irish Oatmeal every morning all winter. I know this is not a "thing," but I do look forward to it each morning. Here's a simple way of cooking steel cut oatmeal. No simmering and watching for 30 minutes, which seems to be an insurmountable amount of time for breakfast eaters. This method delivers oatmeal texture at it's best. When you're first up in the morning, getting your coffee say, bring a cup of water, plus $\frac{1}{8}$ teaspoon salt, to a boil. Add a ¼ cup Irish oatmeal. Turn off the heat just as soon as the mixture has come to a boil (15 seconds) and put a lid on the pan. About the time the oatmeal has reached room temperature, it is ready to be reheated. I fix mine before I go to the Y and it is ready for warming up when I return.

- Cotton napkins for everyday. Find some that can be folded, smoothed and do not have to be ironed. Buy lots, so that you can use them for a crowd.

- My Moleskine Notebook. A newcomer to my list of favorites. We'll see if it lasts. This is a small black flexible notebook in which I write the things I would have formerly written on the back of a deposit slip, never to be seen again. It has a handy attached elastic that keeps it from coming open in your pocketbook. It contains a wealth of important information like book recommendations, names I need to remember, the name of a good, cheap wine, people's email addresses, a recipe or two.

- A battered silver cup (teacup shape) I use as an ice scoop in an ice bucket. I use it in our refrigerator ice bin when it's not on party duty. Sometimes you'll see people use a glass or a plastic cup. Both those things are apt to break and pose some danger. Ice scoops designed for the job are frequently too big for an ice bucket. The cup seems to be the perfect size and shape for filling glasses. Since perfect condition is not what you need, you can probably find one for yourself for not very much money.

- And in the garden, my big scoop-shaped leaf pan (as opposed to dustpan). It's pinkie-finger lightweight, but very durable. I've had mine for years. It's perfect for taking leaves and trimmings to my compost pile. If you want to see what I'm talking about enter "Scoop" and "Henta Products" in the Google search space.

- My grandmother's frog and pond vase. It was definitely not one of the most valued things at my mother's house since I found it on a garage shelf. I mentioned to our son, Pope, that I hoped I could claim it when my brother and I divided our mother's things, and his reply was, "I don't think you'll have any contest!" Well, it could be construed as tacky, but I love it. It's a shallow green "pond shaped" bowl with a frog perched on the side. It's a great solution as a centerpiece when there are few flowers. You can float a blossom or two or three—or even a pretty leaf—and have an appealing "arrangement." Think of it as a water garden for the table.

- My cookbooks. Here's a list I rely on for recipes. Others I love to read, but almost never cook from. *Helen Corbitt's Cookbook*, *Virginia Hospitality*, *The New York Times Cookbook* (the one before the most recent revision), any of the Julia Childs cookbooks, any of Marian Burros's cookbooks, any of the Sunset series of cookbooks, any of the Silver Palate cookbooks. I love *Country Weekends* and the other cookbooks by Lee Bailey, but I haven't cooked out of them in several years. Favorite newcomers are those by Ina Garten, a.k.a. the Barefoot Contessa. Her recipes are easily cooked by the home cook and the pictures, largely featuring Garten and her husband, are charming and make you want to cook food that will make you as happy as they appear! Of course I also use the *Joy of Cooking* (the one before this last revision) and *Fannie Farmer* (the newest revision by Marion Cunningham as well as the revision before that). I also have enjoyed many recipes from *The Good Food Gourmet* by Jane Brody. She has designed healthy recipes, but not too healthy. *The Tassajara Cookbook* has wonderful suggestions for freewheeling vegetarian dishes. I enjoy community cookbooks of all sorts for the picture they give of different locales.

- My favorite cookbooks are easily identifiable. They're all in deplorable condition. *Helen Corbitt* has come completely apart and is in several pieces. I could get a new one but it wouldn't be the cowgirl way. And besides, it has another favorite-cookbook-identifying feature; it has a list of starred recipes written on the flyleaf. This has been helpful when trying to track down a recipe. Now where IS that flyleaf?!

- I've used Helen Corbitt for my whole married life. She was in charge of the Zodiac Room at Neiman Marcus (the mother store) in Dallas. When I was growing up in Arkansas, going there was a wonderful treat when we traveled to Dallas to shop once or twice a year. Her recipes are simplified classics designed for kitchen crews before all restaurant kitchens were filled with graduates of The Culinary Institute of America and of Johnson & Wales. She was way ahead of Martha Stewart in her emphasis on eye appeal. Her recipes are simple and they "turn out."

- Oh, Oh! Here's a new entry to the Favorite Things list that's not so inexpensive! My iPod! I listen to Audiobooks and have more than I want to admit to. Barbara Harbison asked me recently which luxury I enjoy regularly that I would most hate to do without. No question, my iPod Nano, filled at any point with 60 or 70 books.

I urge you to have the pleasure of looking around and noticing your favorite things. I've had a good time thinking about the things in my life that are so useful that every use brings satisfaction. Ask yourself Barbara's question. Her favorite luxury, by the way, is Starbucks, which represents a treat in the day far more important than a cup of coffee.

Frogs can more often be heard than seen at the Cemetery's Lotus Pond.

Apples

Here's a bonus Apple Chapter, all because of Tom Burford, who happens to be local but who is apple expert to the world. Thanks to his quick, eloquent and elegant responses, you have much more here than the apple recipes I planned to include. The apple dishes I frequently make are apple crisps, fried apples and applesauce. Although those dishes would have appeared in the Dessert, Breakfast and Side Dish sections respectively, they appear in this chapter because of Tom's help.

Tom grew up in Virginia apple territory so far deep in Amherst County that there was no school close enough to attend. Later he and his brother were in the nursery business supplying vintage fruit trees all over the world. He knows apples from every angle.

Take note that when Tom gives recipes, he's a purist. He mentions no sweeteners or flavorings. He wants cooks to choose the appropriate apple for the job and to use that apple when it's in its peak form.

Three recipes, one for Apple Toddy, one for Apple Pone (a staple when he was growing up) and one for his favorite Scalloped Potatoes with Apples are recipes which came through Tom and which I am delighted to have in this book.

Tom's soon-to-be-published *Apples of America* will be released by Timber Press in June 2013. He has whittled it down from 1,300 to 800 pages! It could be said that this is Tom's Tome. In spite of its size, knowing Tom, it is sure to be lively reading.

Tom is on hand at the Lynchburg farmers' market most Saturday mornings. He is also kind enough to respond to questions by email with quick and beautiful little essays.

I asked him early one morning for advice for our son, Pope, who had collected a few apples from a White House tree and wanted to try growing trees for his three boys from seeds from those apples. Here is his response:

They are likely Newtown (Albemarle) Pippins and the seeds from the three apples can be extracted and washed and thoroughly dried and then saved until February to be planted. A 3-quart pot will accommodate the three to five seeds from each fruit. In a good planting medium space the seeds around the pot surface and cover about three times the seed size and lightly moisten. Keep the pots in

40° to 65°F covered with a lightly fitting plastic cover and inspect regularly so that they do not get too wet. The label should have the name of the son doing the planting because it will not be a Newtown (Albemarle) Pippin since every seed in every apple is a new variety. The tree will also grow up to be a standard size between 20 and 30 feet. Planting from seeds is very exciting and a horticulture adventure because one never knows the fruit until it is tasted.

Since that response I have heard a lecture given by Tom at the Jones Memorial Library in Lynchburg and learned that there's one chance in 30,000 that seeds from an apple will produce the apples of it's parent tree. That's why we hear so much about grafting in connection with fruit orchards.

International heirloom apple expert Tom Burford

Tom Burford's Apple Toddy

Tom's entertaining recipe for authentic applejack was included in Food to Die For. *I must confess, it was a recipe I did not proof, but I will try Apple Toddy when the fall apples and cider are in. (Later: I did try it and it is potent and delicious!)*

1 Gallon Apple Cider

1 Pint Filtered Water

1 Pint Applejack (available in a liquor store)

Boil the apple cider until the gallon has been reduced to 1 pint. Blend with equal parts filtered water and applejack and enjoy a bracing winter drink.

This recipe appeared in the *Washington Post* in September 2011.

Virginia Apple Pone

Tom Burford lent me a little booklet put out by the Virginia State Horticultural Society in 1915. He directed me to a recipe for Virginia Apple Pone, which his mother made for the Burford dogs. In a note attached, Tom has revealed that the Burford boys frequently beat the dogs to the pone. He says his mother implored, "Please leave some for the dogs!"

Here's the recipe, in case you have dogs or boys who might enjoy Apple Pone.

1 Quart Sweet Apples
1 Pint Boiling Water
1 Quart White Corn Meal
Sweet Milk
2 Tablespoons Sugar
1-2 Teaspoons Salt

Pare apples and chop fine. Pour boiling water over corn meal; when cool, add enough sweet milk to make a soft batter; add sugar, salt and apples. Pour into a well-buttered pan, cover and bake in a moderate oven for 2 hours.

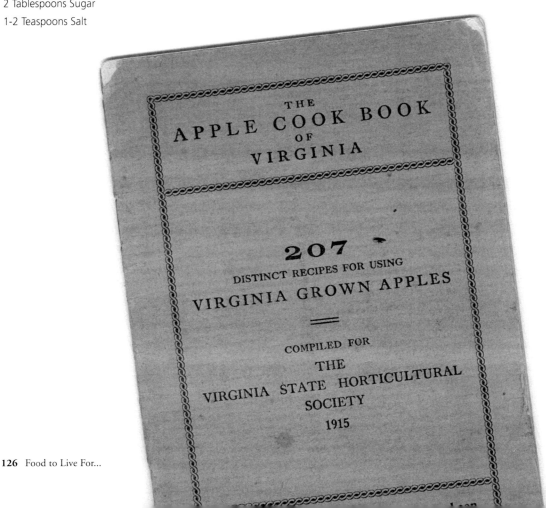

Apple Crisp

When the berries and other fruits of summer have gone, we don't have to wait long for Virginia apples to appear in abundant variety at our farmers' market. For our Saturday breakfasts, we are soon enjoying apple crisps. Like the berry cobblers, they're easy and delicious.

4 Tart Apples (I usually use Winesaps), sliced but left unpeeled

1 Cup Sugar, divided

Nutmeg and Cinnamon, to taste

4 Tablespoons Water

½ Cup Butter

½ Teaspoon Salt

1 Cup Flour

Preheat oven to 350 degrees. Place apples in a buttered, 9-inch square baking dish. Sprinkle apples with ½ cup sugar, nutmeg, cinnamon and water. With an electric mixer, cream butter, remaining sugar and salt. Add flour and mix well. Pat flour mixture over apples and bake for 30–40 minutes.

Serves 6.

The phosphorous in APPLES renews the nerve forces.

teaspoonful salt, 1-2 teaspoonful soda, 1 teaspoonful cream of tartar or 4 level teaspoonfuls baking powder, milk enough to mix quite soft, 3 apples, pared and sliced. Mix in order given, bake in a shallow cake pan 30 minutes.

APPLE SAUCE CAKE No. 1.

1 cup sugar, 1-2 cup shortening, 1-2 teaspoonful cloves, 1 teaspoonful cinnamon, 1-4 teaspoonful salt, 1 cup chopped raisins dredged in flour, 1 teaspoonful soda dissolved in warm water, 1 cup sour apple sauce, 1 3-4 cups flour.

Cream sugar and shortening. Add other ingredients in order given. Add soda dissolved in water to unsweetened apple sauce and beat all together, add flour lastly. Bake in a loaf about 45 minutes.

APPLE SAUCE CAKE No. 2.

1 cup unsweetened apple sauce, 1 1-2 cups flour, 1-2 cup butter, 1 teaspoonful cinnamon, 1-2 teaspoonful grated nutmeg, yolk of 1 egg, 1-2 teaspoonful soda, 1 teaspoonful baking powder, 2 cups flour.

Strain apple sauce and stir in soda; cream shortening and sugar and add flour sifted with baking powder and spices; beat well and bake in a moderate oven.

APPLE SAUCE CAKE. No. 3.

1 cup butter, 2 cups sugar, 4 eggs, 3 cups flour, 1 1-2 teaspoonfuls baking powder, 1 cup milk, 6 apples, 3-4 cup sugar, 1 teaspoonful butter.

Cream sugar and butter, add 2 eggs at a time, beating hard; sift flour and baking powder, add to milk and mix into a batter. Bake in jelly cake tins. Have apples peeled and sliced, and cook with sugar; when soft rub through a fine sieve, and add butter. When cold use to spread between layers. Cover cake well with sugar sifted over top.

APPLE TEA CAKE.

1 pint flour, 1-2 teaspoonful salt, 3 teaspoonfuls baking powder, 1-4 teaspoonful cinnamon, 2 tablespoonfuls sugar, 1 tablespoonful butter, 1 eggs, 1 scant cup milk, 5 medium sized apples.

Mix and sift dry ingredients. Work in butter and milk gradually and egg well beaten. Spread in well buttered baking pans. Cut apples in eighths or sixteenths and stick in the dough. Sprinkle sugar and cin over the top. Bake in a mod

---

You cannot eat too many APPLES.

CANNED APPLES.

Wipe, quarter, core and pare apples, then weigh. Make a syrup by boiling for 10 minutes 1-3 their weight in sugar with water, allowing 2 1-2 cups to each pound of sugar. Cook apples in syrup until soft, doing a few at a time. Fill jars and seal.

CANNED APPLES AND PINEAPPLE.

4 pounds apples, 4 pounds pineapples, 2 pounds sugar, 2 pints water, rind of 4 lemons.

Pare, core and cut the apples in rings. Cut pineapple in slices, remove skin and eyes, and cut pulp into squares, being careful to reject the core. Boil sugar and water 5 minutes; add pineapple; cook until tender; then cook apples until tender; add lemon rind; fill jars (which have been sterilized) with apple and pineapple, adjust rings, fill jars with syrup, adjust covers and seal.

APPLE CATSUP.

1 cup sugar, 1 teaspoonful pepper, 1 teaspoonful cloves, 1 teaspoonful mustard, 2 teaspoonfuls cinnamon, 2 medium size onions chopped fine, 1 tablespoonful salt, 1 pint vinegar.

Peel and quarter tart apples and stew until soft, in as little water as possible, and pass through a sieve. To each quart of sifted apple add above ingredients. Stir all together and boil 1 hour; bottle while hot; seal very tight. It should be of the same consistency as tomato catsup.

APPLE CHARLOTTE No. 1.

1-3 box of gelatine, 1-3 cup cold water, 1-3 cup boiling water, 1 cup sugar, juice of 1 lemon, 1 cup strained unsweetened apple sauce, whites of 3 eggs.

Line a mold with lady fingers. Soak gelatine in cold water until soft. Pour on the boiling water, add sugar and lemon juice; strain and add apple sauce. Cool in a pan of ice water. Beat the egg whites stiff, and when mixture in mold begins to harden beat together until stiff enough to stand. Pour into mold and set in ice box. Serve with boiled custard made with 3 egg yolks, 1-4 cup sugar, 1 pint milk, salt and vanilla.

APPLE CHARLOTTE No. 2.

8 slices of bread, 1-2 cu

Applesauce

5 Tart Apples

Core and chunk apples. Leave peel on. Place in a heavy-bottomed saucepan over lowest heat. Cover and cook for about 15 minutes. Remove cover and continue to cook, stirring frequently, for another 30 minutes or until apples are soft. Put through a food mill. The peels will be left behind in the mill.

The resulting applesauce will be rosy and, if you have used flavorful apples, will be delicious. Serve warm.

Serves 4.

Hillside Garden Club members enjoy box lunches beneath the shady willow tree beside the Lotus Pond.

Charlotte Shelton's Apple Scalloped Potatoes

This is a superb recipe that comes from Charlotte Shelton, a great friend to Tom Burford. Charlotte and her family own Ablemarle CiderWorks where they make hard cider from heritage apples. Your guests will love these potatoes, but few of them will be able to identify the mystery ingredient.

Unsalted Butter, for dish

2 Pounds Potatoes (preferably Yukon Gold), peeled and sliced

1 Cup Heavy Cream

1 Cup Half and Half

2 Teaspoon Chicken Bouillon Granules

½ Teaspoon Freshly Ground Black Pepper

1 Medium Tart Apple, cored, peeled and thinly diced

1 Cup Grated Gruyère Cheese

Preheat oven to 350 degrees. Generously grease a 3-quart baking dish with butter.

In a large saucepan, combine the potatoes, creams, bouillon and black pepper. Bring the mixture to a simmer and cook, stirring, until liquid thickens slightly.

Pour half of potato mixture into the prepared pan. Scatter diced apple on top. Add remaining potatoes. Press down to submerge potatoes; add more cream if necessary. Sprinkle with cheese. Bake until golden and potatoes are tender, 45 minutes to 1 hour.

Serves 6–8.

Fried Apples

The basic directions for these apples come from that wonderful cook, Edna Lewis, in The Taste of Country Cooking. *I've altered it a little, because I like the peels left on. Suit yourself. Edna peeled hers.*

6 Apples, cut into bite-sized chunks

3 Tablespoons Bacon Fat (or Butter if you don't happen to have bacon fat)

⅓ Cup Sugar

Heat fat in skillet over medium-high heat until sizzling. Add apples, cover and cook until they soften and release juices. Remove cover from pan and sprinkle sugar over the apples. Cook with the cover off, stirring frequently, until the apples have begun to brown.

Serves 4–6.

When I was writing down this recipe, I sent a very early-morning email to Tom Burford, asking him to name the best apples for frying. I told him that I was using Edna Lewis's instructions. This is his rewarding reply:

My friend, Edna, whom I miss and still want to ask a thousand questions, preferred the Stayman for frying. I would send Stayman apples and creecy salad to her in Atlanta (I have always put two Es in creecy. Do you know the usual spelling?) She said peeling the apples made the dish more frothy.

The Burfords' apple of choice was Grimes Golden, fully ripe when the sugar is very high. We annually would freeze 100 quarts for winter use, slicing them into the bag and quickly freezing. In a very heavy-bottomed Cuisinart pan that I still use, a frozen package is dumped and lidded on high heat for a few minutes; then, turned to medium high and chunked up and re-lidded, checked every five minutes or so until the desired degree of cooking is reached. Some will add some butter in the pan when they are first broken up, but I like the apples alone on buttered biscuits from the oven. My urban visitors would always ask me to cook a second pan. My mother always cooked two pans of apples, intending one to be for the next meal, but both were eaten and then she, at the next meal, cooked two more and they were eaten too.

130 Food to Live For...

Other notable apples for frying are Yellow Transparent, Lodi, Red Astrachan, Early Harvest, Smokehouse, Virginia Beauty, York and Winesap.

The quintessential frying apple is Magnum Bonum, the superstar of frying apples of the late-19th and early-20th centuries. The tree is highly susceptible to cedar apple rust which will destroy a spray-unprotected tree in a few years. When a Commonwealth of Virginia law was repealed in the 1930s that permitted the orchardist the right to remove the host cedar trees on his neighbors' property, Magnum Bonum disappeared. Vintage Virginia Apples grow a few for their own and my use and I will try to remember to bring you a mess.

Artists of all media are frequently seen capturing the unique beauty of the Cemetery grounds.

Thanksgiving

I've often looked around the grocery store Thanksgiving week and wondered why so many people are there. There are people lined up at every checkout. Why do they have such anxious expressions on their faces? National emergency is in the air! Why this storming of the market when only one in about eight people is going to be hosting Thanksgiving dinner? If ever there was a time of communal living, Thanksgiving is it! What are all those people doing in the grocery store when most of them will be eating away from home? Charley Hurt told me at the Y this morning that it's a fever.

In spite of teeming supermarkets, Thanksgiving is a superb holiday. Christmas should try to be more like Thanksgiving. Families together, but no presents, no obligatory decorations, no thinking up a menu. Tolerance and civility of all family members, even the most cantankerous, is expected. Good table manners are required. Contribution to the conversation is the only obligation. Actually embracing elderly relatives, and enduring it cheerfully, is also a requirement.

Peter and I hosted the greater Ward family Thanksgiving for years. It was finally necessary for Peter to drive the geriatric Cadillac onto our lawn to deposit at the front door those who could no longer make it up our difficult walk. I love looking at the pictures of those years. We had a great many elderly Wards. Those needing a seat on the front row for the annual picture grew year by year until those requiring assistance and the able-bodied ones standing behind were in about equal numbers.

Seat Children with Adults

The family included several children who always wanted to be seated at their own table. Every year they would send an emissary from the under-twelve ranks to ask if they could sit together. And every year, I said, "No." I made them sit amongst the elderly, feeling dining amongst the relatives of all ages was good for all concerned. And besides, it would provide short story material forever.

Seating the adults was always a challenge. I had table arrangements, and then I had fantasy table arrangements, which I can't tell you about here. Suffice it to say that Peter's aunts loved men! I always seated the aunt who had suffered a stroke by one of the acquired (in-law) husbands whom she particularly enjoyed.

Take Annual Pictures of the Gathering

Now Thanksgiving has shifted to other relatives' homes and tables and I'm a bit sorry. I look at the annual Thanksgiving pictures—always with a child seated on the ground in front with a large sign declaring the year—and feel a bit melancholy when I realize that the whole row of seated elderly relatives is gone. Soon our generation will be seated for the picture. And the child with the "year" sign will be cooking the turkey.

Jane and Kenneth White have a restored cabin in the country outside Appomatox. They spend many weekends and sometimes weeks at a time there. It is also a place for family gatherings. This last Thanksgiving, they had their two "out-of-town" children, Spence and Gena, and their families, for the long weekend. This included Gena's husband's brother and his family. Isn't that the nice thing about Thanksgiving? Your extended family can become more extended!

Jane and Kenneth's son-in-law, Bill O'Keefe, was chief cook, although everybody shared kitchen duty. I thought it would be fun to know what staples Jane thought necessary for 16 people for the four days. This is her list in case you need a checklist for a similar occasion!

She starts with a list of standard items:

Coffee

Tea

Paper products (towels, napkins, cups, toilet paper)

Sugar

Honey

Sweeta

Flour

Salad dressing

Laundry detergent

Dishwasher detergent

And especially for the Thanksgiving weekend crowd she bought:

Beer and wine

Juices

Milk

Butter

Eggs

Baggies (3 sizes)

Lemonade mix

Nuts

Cereals (including Mueslix and Cheerios)

Oatmeal

Cranberry sauce

Mayonnaise

Bread (including sandwich bread and French bread)

Homemade rolls

English muffins

Pepperidge Farm herb dressing

Parmesan cheese

Fruit cake

Bacon (cooked and ready for microwave)

Sausage patties (cooked and ready for microwave)

Spaghetti sauce and noodles

18-pound turkey

Homemade corn salad

1 quart chicken salad

1 pint hommade pimiento cheese

1 quart raw oysters

Seaport cocktail sauce for oysters

Clementines

Bananas

Canapés

Homemade applesauce

Gravy base from Williams-Sonoma

Without knowing any more about the family holiday than this list, don't you get a picture of a happy, memorable weekend?

Afterword

If you've read this far in this book, you'll know how very much I enjoy cooking and eating. Even more, you'll know how I much enjoy food with my friends. You've probably noticed that many of the recipes contained in this book are those of my family and friends.

Food is a strong connector with people we care about. For me, many of those people are a part of my life in Lynchburg where we've lived for thirty-five years. Others are part of my past lives in Prescott and Texarkana and Richmond and Washington. I associate many of the things I cook with many people from several decades. Most are still alive, but some are not.

Almost every recipe in this book allows me to channel friends and family into my kitchen to keep me company. As wonderful as old photos and pictures can be, the very best way to keep friends alive and present is through food. I think of my grandmother, whom I did not know, when I cook Mur's Peas (in *Food to Die For*). I think of my cousin, Bod, and the hot, hot peppers and fun she brought to family reunions when I make White Gazpacho. Almost every recipe comes with associations.

I hope you'll enjoy these recipes and that you are building your own food connections and memories. I like to think that someone whom I do not even know will be cooking a dish that my grandmother cooked and that he or she will know the recipe's genealogy. That means that my grandmother and I will be there, too.

Cooks in the Gravegarden
By Ted Delaney

Vendors and buyers at the Lynchburg City Market, 1100 block of Main Street, circa 1890
Courtesy of Virginia Historical Society

Judy Rieves
1814–1887

Judy Rieves is one of the earliest known African American food vendors in Lynchburg. She was the proprietress (sometimes "huckstress") of a "Snack House" at the Lynchburg City Market for several years in the 1870s and 80s. One city directory gave her work address as "Eating House Stall No. 60" at the City Market.

Judy died in 1887 and was buried in the Old City Cemetery. Her church club, the Mt. Lebanon Society of Jackson Street Methodist Church, helped pay for her burial and erect her tombstone. As a businesswoman with assets, but no will, her estate was appraised by court order. The inventory consisted almost entirely of the contents of her Snack House.

Who knows what delicious things came forth from this cookware and equipment?

1 large cooking stove & utensils	$10.00
1 small stove	1.75
1 dozen spoons	.25
1 dipper	.05
2 oil cans	.30
1 churn	.40
2 small lamps	.20
9 coffee pots	.90
3 soup bowls	.30
10 vegetable dishes	.50
4 soap dishes	.20
9 tea cups	.45
1 lamp	.40
1 bench	.25
1 milk bucket	.25
1 sugar bucket	.10
3 tables	.75
2 pudding plates	.20
3 stone pots	.75
1 glass jar	.20
6 cake stands	1.50
1 sugar dish	.15
4 glasses	.20
1 set of castors	.50
5 meat dishes	1.50
13 plates	.50
3 chairs	.75
1 table	.25
1 meat block	.25
1 safe	1.25
9 waiters	1.35
Total	$26.40

Amelia Perry Pride
1857–1932

"I believe in training the head, heart, and hand."

Amelia Pride is best known as the longtime elementary school teacher and principal whose name lives on today in the Lynchburg City Schools' "Pride Center." Few people know she also trained an entire generation of African American cooks in Lynchburg in the early 20th century.

Amelia Perry was born to free black parents in Lynchburg just before the Civil War. She attended Hampton Institute in the 1870s, where she developed her lifelong passion for vocational or "industrial" education. She believed she could uplift her race by teaching the practical, hands-on skills of sewing, cooking, cleaning, conservation, and thrift—what we call "home economics" today. She believed knowledge of these basic domestic skills, which so many former slaves and their children did not have, was the first rung on the ladder out of poverty and dependence.

In 1903 Amelia established the Theresa Pierce Cooking School at 904 Madison Street, in a small brick house she owned across the street from her own home. The school was named in memory of the young daughter of Mr. S. S. Pierce of Boston, Massachusetts, whose financial gift made the school possible.

Her granddaughter Miriam Pride Kyle remembered, "Her purpose was to train [the students] to professionally cook and serve and demand a real wage and no longer 'tote left-overs' " back home to their families.

In the 1916-17 academic year Amelia transferred the equipment and supplies of the school to Virginia Theological Seminary and College in Lynchburg's southern suburbs. It became part of the school's teacher training curriculum and was included in the academic catalogue. She also convinced Lynchburg

Courtesy of Hampton University Archives

138 Food to Live For...

City School Superintendent E. C. Glass to make home economics a compulsory course in the black public schools. To honor this legacy, the School Board named the home economics building at Dunbar High School after her in 1949. Although the high school has been torn down, the "Amelia Pride Center" still stands.

Amelia is buried in the Old City Cemetery with her husband Claiborne G. Pride and three sons.

VIRGINIA THEOLOGICAL SEMINARY AND COLLEGE   77

Theresa Pierce Cooking School

DOMESTIC SCIENCE DEPARTMENT

Mrs. AMELIA E. P. PRIDE, Principal
SARA F. TYLER, Instructor

Through the generous spirit of Mrs. A. E. P. Pride, who conducted for fifteen years the Theresa Pierce Cooking School, in the city, a memorial of Miss Theresa Pierce by her father, the same has been transferred to the institution, thereby providing a well-equipped domestic sciene department. All Normals are required to take the full outline course in domestic science.

A well-ordered home is the most sacred altar of society. The proper care of the home is everything in family life. This department aims to give a thorough working and teaching knowledge of the domestic art.

First Year—Care of Kitchen, Use of Gas and Coal Ranges; Special Study of Measuring of Ingredients and Methods of Combining; Theory and Practice of Cooking Cereals; Care and Preparation of Vegetables; Beverages, and How to Serve Them.

Second Year. Theory and Practice of Breadmaking; Baking Powder and Baking Powder Mixtures; Household Economics; Special Study of Care and Preparation of Meats; Special Training as Waitress and Hostess; Theory and Practice of Cake Baking.

Third Year—Invalid Cooking; Marketing; Advanced Lessons in Serving and Waiting; Specialty of Pastry, Desserts, Entrees and Salads.

Fourth Year—Making of Menus and Well-Balanced Dietaries; Preparation of Course Dinners; General Housekeeping; Practice Teaching.

Course of study of the cooking program established by Amelia Pride, from the 1920-21 Virginia Theological Seminary and College Catalogue
Courtesy of OCC/SMA

Georges Blanc-Hector
1907–1987

Georges Blanc-Hector was a highly respected French chef, best known as the executive chef of the Waldolf-Astoria Hotel in New York in the 1950s and 60s.

Georges was a born in Mont Plancher, Haute-Saône, in eastern France near the Swiss border. When Georges was 10 years old, his father, who was a chef by profession, was killed in World War I. The French government apprenticed him and other war orphans to the chefs of the Grand Hôtel Continental in Paris. They lived in the attic of the hotel, and spent their days in the kitchen learning the basics of cooking.

The young Georges must have shown great promise. After being hired to work as a cook aboard France's flagship ocean liner, the *Île de France*, in the late 1920s, he became the personal chef of France's World War I general Marshal Joseph Joffre. Georges later found work in New York City, where he met his wife Lucette and earned the coveted position of executive chef of the Waldorf-Astoria Hotel.

Georges was a member of the Académie Culinaire de France, Maîtres Cuisiniers de France, and Société Culinaire Philanthropique.

He and Lucette retired to Warm Springs, Virginia, in the 1970s. They eventually moved to Westminster Canterbury in Lynchburg, where Georges died in 1987 and Lucette in 2001. Upon her death, their ashes were mixed together and spread in the Cemetery's Scatter Garden.

As Executive Chef of the Waldorf-Astoria Hotel in New York, George Blanc-Hector judged the Madison Square Boys' Club Annual Cooking Contest in 1959.

Photos courtesy of OCC/SMA

Special thanks to Bob Morrison and Alex and Maithé Ardrey

Emily Clements Jefferson
1845–1920

As the keeper of a tavern just across the river from Lynchburg, "Aunt Emily" Jefferson was well-known in the city for her exceptional cooking and hospitality.

Emily was born a slave in Fluvanna County. According to family oral history, her mother was a Cherokee Indian, from whom she inherited her straight black hair and habit of not wearing shoes.

After the Civil War her husband Henry ran a livery stable at the end of the toll bridge leading from the foot of Ninth Street in downtown Lynchburg to what is now Madison Heights. Nearby was an old inn that Emily kept. Her obituary recalled that "many horseback parties, sometimes fresh from a fox hunt, would enjoy her carefully prepared breakfasts. During the influenza epidemic, pans of hot biscuits came from the latticed doorway of 'Aunt' Emily's house to the needy sufferers, colored and white alike, and she was known to nearly everybody in Amherst county."

Emily was particularly well-known as a "first class cook." The local newspaper once noted that "her famous cooking, especially her 'yeast-powder' biscuit, was sought by the connoisseur of southern cooking."

Jefferson died in 1920 and was buried in her family plot in the Old City Cemetery. Although her grave is unmarked, the Jefferson plot is easily located by the prominent "Kneeling Angel" monument, which marks the grave of Emily's infant grandson Emmett.

Courtesy of Gregory Jefferson

Emily Jefferson's son Thomas remembered that Gen. William Mahone—the famous railroad executive, politician, and one-time resident of Lynchburg—never left town without first buying a loaf of his mother's salt rising bread.

Courtesy of Library of Congress

Cooks in the Gravegarden **141**

Lucinda Twyman
1851–1918

Lucinda Twyman was the personal cook for two generations of the Moore family in Lynchburg. She represents the countless African American women who cooked for Lynchburgers—black and white—throughout the 19th and 20th centuries, and many of whom are buried in the Old City Cemetery.

In the 1910 Lynchburg city directory, out of nearly 4,000 total African American workers, over 300 are given the occupation of "cook." The vast majority were women, and more than half "lived in" with a white family, either in the residence itself or in a rear dependency.

Around 1890 Lucinda began cooking for tobacconist Israel Snead Moore and his wife Cornelia. They lived at 310 Washington Street, in the fashionable Diamond Hill neighborhood. When Israel and Cornelia moved to Easton Avenue (in the Rivermont "suburbs") around 1905, Lucinda stayed on Diamond Hill and cooked for their son Maurice Moore and his wife Mary at 606 Pearl Street.

Nettie Terrell Moore remembered that "The servants were an integral part of our family life." The two "best beloved" servants were "our peerless Mammy," Anica Mitchell, and "honest, loyal Cindy, quick of wit and ready of tongue," referring to Lucinda Twyman.

Lucinda died in 1918 and was buried in the Old City Cemetery. She rests beside her sister-in-law and fellow Moore family servant Anica Mitchell, who died the year before.

Lucinda "Cindy" Twyman cooked for two generations of the Moore family on Diamond Hill.

Courtesy of Jones Memorial Library

The Pat Mathews Dinner Party
Edited by Ted Delaney

The Pat Mathews Dinner Party, held on the afternoon of New Year's Day, 1868, was the most celebrated meal in Lynchburg history. It was reported in both the New York Times *and* New York Tribune*, and an innovative photography studio in Lynchburg even copyrighted a collage of portraits of the host and his 18 invited guests.*

The ambitious menu was matched by the grandiose prose of a nameless newspaper reporter, whose article from the Lynchburg Daily Virginian*, January 2, 1868, is excerpted here.*

The Host
Patrick Mathews
1783–1870
Merchant

An event took place in this city yesterday, the like of which few men have ever seen. It was a social reunion of the oldest citizens of the place—a gathering of the patriarchs around the festive board. So much of years, of worth and of wisdom, have seldom been grouped together in one collection.

The occasion of the assemblage was a New Year's dinner given by Mr. Patrick Mathews, an aged citizen, to his venerable friends and contemporaries of the city who had attained the age of seventy-five, of whom there were eighteen on the list, exclusive of himself.

It was indeed an interesting sight to see assembled together around the same board so much of age, wisdom and ripe experience—so many who have been spared beyond the period allotted to man. What crowding emotions

"Strict and exacting of others in all business relations, he has not been less scrupulous in the exactness with which he has accorded to them all their just rights. At the end of a business life covering many millions of dollars, we suppose there is no man who can truthfully say he has suffered wrong at his hands."

must have come upon them—what a flood of reminiscences must have flowed into their memories! So many companions of youth, of manhood, of riper years, and of advanced old age met together in social re-union, is an event well calculated to touch the sensibilities, to stir up the recollections, and to awaken tender emotions in the breasts of the participants. How many thousand who sat out on the journey of life with them have fallen by the way—how many loved friends have they been called on to surrender to the inexorable messenger!

What a panorama of stirring events in the world's history has passed since they came on the stage of existence! Empires have risen and fallen; thrones have been established and overturned; wars have deluged the earth with blood; great heroes have risen, flourished and passed away; the arts and sciences have made rapid strides; railroads, telegraphs and gas lights have been invented; the earth has been girded with electric thought; and in all departments of human skill, energy and achievement great changes have been wrought. And even coming down to a more circumscribed sphere, how has this town, with which they have been so long identified, changed and grown within their recollection, and how often its population has been metamorphosed. The modest town, then but little more than a "Ferry," has grown into a respectable city, and spread itself over hills that were covered with chinquapin bushes when they were boys. To that growth many of them have contributed in no small degree.

As we looked upon the little circle of Lynchburg octogenarians, seated at the festive board, a feeling tinged with sadness came over our heart, as we thought of the brief space of human existence, at its longest time. In the language of the monarch bard of Israel, "*it is soon cut off, and we fly away.*" But it is glorious to see the patriarch and patriot of more than fourscore years going calmly towards the sunset of life, with the prospect of "resting under the shade of the trees on the other side of the cold river," whose *hither* bank marks the boundaries of time, and whose opposite shore skirts the spirit land.

The Meeting
Between one and two o'clock the company assembled at the residence of Mr. Mathews, on Church Street. All were present except [Messrs. McDonald and Shoemaker]. The greetings were cordial and warm between the veteran friends of years standing. An hour or more was spent in free and social conversation, in which many pleasant reminiscences were indulged in and incidents related. In this way the time was spent agreeably until

The Dinner
was announced. On repairing to the dining room, a sumptuous repast was found awaiting them. Mr. Mathews took the head of the table, and Bishop Early was requested to preside at the foot, which he did with his accustomed readiness and dignity. A handsomely printed bill of fare was laid at each

plate. Each course of the sumptuous spread was taken in its order, in which the guests did full justice to the bounteous hospitality of their host. All seemed to eat with relish the good things set before them, and to enjoy the repast with a hearty relish.

Toasts and Speeches
After the cloth was removed wine and coffee were brought on, and toasts and speeches indulged in. We regret that we have not a verbatim report of what was said.

The health of the host was proposed by Bishop Early and duly responded to by the company. Maj. Garland replied for Mr. Mathews, whose infirm health would not permit him to speak. Maj. Garland spoke of the remarkable character of the meeting—the number of so advanced age that were permitted to assemble together—of the appropriateness of their meeting in this pleasant way, and expressed the fear that it was the last time that all of them would enjoy the privilege of coming together, but hoped it would not be.

Mr. Edley proposed the memory of the late Alexander Liggat, of the firm of Liggat & Mathews, which existed here more than half a century ago. Drank in silence.

Mr. Edley also offered the health of Rev. Mr. Labby—a good citizen, magistrate, husband, father, etc., which was properly honored by the assemblage. Mr. Labby did not reply.

Bishop Early made some feeling remarks about the meeting together of so many aged men—of their long business careers, temperate habits, etc.

He indulged in some moral reflections, in a few words; but seeming to be overcome by his feelings and crowding emotions resumed his seat.

Mr. George Percival offered (but did not *drink* to it:)

"May the wheels of friendship never run dry for the want of grease."

Mr. Hardy proposed the following:—

"The present Company: Venerable relic of a purer and better age; May their descendants live to see the day when Virginia will be what Virginia was."

Mr. Edley made some suitable remarks, and proposed the health of Mr. McDonald which was responded to in the usual way by the company.

A toast, proposed by Mr. Edley, was drank to the memory of the late Mr. Jesse Hare.

Maj. Garland offered the health of the skillful physician, to whom he owed his life, and true gentleman, Dr. Owens.

After the toast was drank, the Doctor replied briefly. He was the oldest citizen of the place—that is had lived here longer than any other resident. He was gratified at the sentiment which had been drank. He cordially reciprocated the good wishes extended to him. He had not practiced the art of public speaking, and begged to be excused.

An effort was here made to adjourn. The

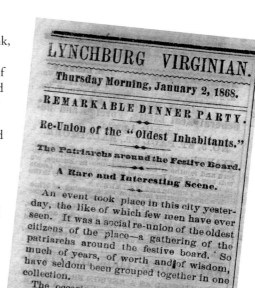

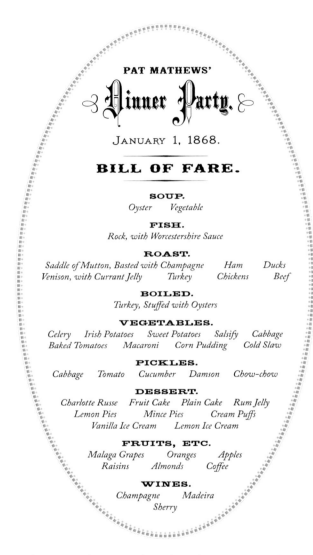

PAT MATHEWS'
Dinner Party.
JANUARY 1, 1868.

BILL OF FARE.

SOUP.
Oyster   Vegetable

FISH.
Rock, with Worcestershire Sauce

ROAST.
Saddle of Mutton, Basted with Champagne   Ham   Ducks
Venison, with Currant Jelly   Turkey   Chickens   Beef

BOILED.
Turkey, Stuffed with Oysters

VEGETABLES.
Celery   Irish Potatoes   Sweet Potatoes   Salsify   Cabbage
Baked Tomatoes   Macaroni   Corn Pudding   Cold Slaw

PICKLES.
Cabbage   Tomato   Cucumber   Damson   Chow-chow

DESSERT.
Charlotte Russe   Fruit Cake   Plain Cake   Rum Jelly
Lemon Pies   Mince Pies   Cream Puffs
Vanilla Ice Cream   Lemon Ice Cream

FRUITS, ETC.
Malaga Grapes   Oranges   Apples
Raisins   Almonds   Coffee

WINES.
Champagne   Madeira
Sherry

"It is not to be wondered at that so tempting an array of good things provoked the appetites of the guests to unusual performances. They were at the table more than two hours, not eating all the time, however."

Bishop said he saw some younger friends at the door, and thought it was cruel to keep them from the good dinner that was awaiting. In this the lookers-on strenuously objected, and the sitting was protracted a while longer, during which a good deal of pleasantry was indulged in.

At length Judge Wilson rose and said, that he had observed there were seventeen of them at the table, and that all were Virginians and Irishmen—thirteen of the former and four of the latter. He proposed that they drink a toast to Ireland and Virginia, and then adjourn that others might take their places at the table. The toast was hastily responded to; the Bishop pronounced the benediction, and then the company rose and retired from the room.

After a little general conversation, the honored guests left for their homes, each taking with him a memento of the event.

It was indeed a memorable occasion. "Take it all in all, we ne'er shall see its like again."

After the old folks had retired Mr. D. T. C. Peters, who resides with Mr. Mathews, entertained a large number of his friends in elegant style.

The smooth and agreeable manner in which everything passed off was the subject of general comment.

Great credit is due to Mr. D. T. C. Peters, Mr. Jas. M. Booker, and still more, to Mrs. Booker, who lent her kind and invaluable assistance, for the thoroughness and excellence of the preparations, and for the pleasant and prompt manner in which all the guests were served and entertained.

The entertainment by Mr. Peters to his friends, after the seniors had left, was of a delightful and convivial character. The intermingling of friends, of whom there were thirty or forty, was cordial and joyous. Glasses were pledged in hearty faith, songs were sung, jests passed around the board, and jollity reigned supreme. Some of the singing was splendid, especially the Irish songs, which drew the venerable host from his bed, to which he had retired, back to the dining room, and one of them, the Irish Emigrant's Lament, caused tears to flow down his cheeks. We trust there may be many recurrences of the happy events on New Year's Day.

Tanner and Van Ness's *Pat Mathews' Dinner Party* collage was copyrighted and sold for $5 unframed and $7 framed.

Courtesy of Lynchburg Museum System

**Bishop John Early
1786–1873**
Methodist Bishop

"In the social circle he is agreeable, and often entertains his friends with anecdotes, and pleasant reminiscences of other days. He is always courteous in his bearing; entertains with old Virginia hospitality; and spreads cheerfulness around him in whatever circle he is thrown."

**Judge Daniel A. Wilson
1792–1873**
Lawyer and Judge

"Contrary to his wishes the people elected him to the Legislature in 1824, and he continued to serve in that body until he was elected to the Governor's Council in 1829. He occupied that position for a period of about ten years, under three Governors, viz: Governors Giles, Floyd (the elder) and Tazwell. Twice during the time he was Lieutenant Governor, and once acting Governor of the State during the protracted absence of the Governor."

Maj. James Garland
1792–1885
Commonwealth's Attorney

"Maj. Garland is a strong, vigorous and sometimes powerful speaker; and in old party times his clarion voice often rallied the "unwashed" legions of Democracy to the charge. He remains in stout and unimpaired health; and claims he can out run and throw down any man in the party."

John G. Meem
1794–1873
"Oldest merchant in the city"
City Councilman,
Bank President, and
Railroad Director

"Though well advanced in years, he shows no signs of age; and his remarkable physique and fine personal appearance are the subject of general comment and admiration. We don't know any young man in town, aspiring for the smiles of beauty, who approaches him in good looks, if he will pardon us for saying it."

Dr. William Owen
c. 1786–1875
Physician

"The Doctor's name is, and has been probably for half a century, a house-hold word in the homes of Lynchburg; and he was never more welcome to them than now. He is a model of the skillful physician, the kind-hearted man, and the old Virginia gentleman."

David R. Edley
c. 1792–1875
"the Nestor of the Lynchburg bar"
"the oldest member of the legal profession in the city"

"He is a fine talker and a most interesting companion, especially when in reminiscent vein. With a cheerful and genial temperament, and a strong predilection towards the witty and humorous, he is in the habit of viewing matters in their pleasantest and brightest aspect and so presenting them to others. His nature does not partake of the sombre and lugubrious."

Albon McDaniel
1786–1870
Commission Merchant, Councilman, Alderman, and Mayor

"He moved to Nashville in 1841, making the journey on horseback in seventeen days. He remained there until the end of the war, when he returned to Lynchburg by rail, being the first and last time he ever traveled on a railroad."

James McDonald, Sr.
c. 1790–1870
Farmer, Miller, and Tobacconist

"His life has been one of many vicissitudes, and he has realized the fickleness of fortune in its varied and varying aspects, now dispensing worldly prosperity and now adversity."

"Uncle George" Percival, Sr.
1792–1877
Merchant and Temperance Leader

"With a Roman firmness, however, are mingled in him the generous and ennobling traits and impulses of his countrymen; and no man is more ready to do a kindly act than he. A veteran in the temperance cause, he has labored long and accomplished much towards reclaiming his fellows from the thralldom of the worst of human enemies."

James Fretwell
1793–1876
Shoe and Boot Maker

"Mr. Fretwell is a man of originality and distinctive character. Though in active business, he is almost a recluse in his habits. He is seldom seen on the streets, except in direct line from his store to his home. He does not meddle with affairs of others, nor is it exactly prudent for others to meddle with his. But beneath a rugged exterior he wears a kind heart and sterling principles."

Pleasant Labby
1792–1869
Tobacconist and Universalist Preacher

"Mr. Labby is a believer in the Universalists' faith, and a preacher in that church: Up to within a year or two past it has been his custom to, occasionally, hold public services in the city. He is a conscientious and upright man, and through a long life has borne himself without reproach."

Buried in Old City Cemetery

Thomas Ferguson
1789–1870
Tobacconist

Michael Connell, Sr.
c. 1792–1888
Merchant

Chesley Hardy
1791–1880
Chair Maker

"Like so many other Lynchburgers, his energies have mainly been devoted to the prosecution of the tobacco business, in which he has been eminently successful, and is so fortunate as to have laid up large wealth for his declining days, as well as the " 'riches in Heaven which neither moth nor rust can corrupt.' "

"He is a frank, blunt, plain-spoken Irishman, and by his correct deportment has secured the respect of the community in which his home has been for so many years. His cheerful and humorous disposition has not been blunted by the touch of time."

"In a life of singular purity, simplicity and modesty, Mr. Hardy has eminently illustrated that 'noblest work of God'—'an honest man.' Unscathed by reproach and untarnished by suspicion, he has passed with white garments through the trials and temptations of the earthly pilgrimage."

James V. Knight
1796–1874
Tobacconist

"Mr. Knight is a quiet, unobtrusive citizen, and bares good repute among his fellows."

Absolem Williams
1788–1869
Tailor

"He served his country in the war of 1812–15, at the termination of which he came to Lynchburg to reside, where he has since lived an irreproachable life, and is widely esteemed for his many virtues."

Warren Gannaway
1790–1875
Tobacconist

"He is a tobacconist by profession; and modestly and quietly has pursued his way of life, without deviating from the strict line of rectitude."

Lindsey Shoemaker
1785–1868
Carpenter

"…has preserved his integrity through the long life he has been permitted to live."

Special Thanks to Pat Dalton, Doug Harvey, and Laura Lembas

Food Index

A

Al Chambers's Mother's Watercress
   Sandwiches 2
Almond Macaroons 107
and Prosciutto Pasta Dish 39
Apple Crisp 127
Apple Pie, Wistar Nelligan's 106
Apple Pone, Virginia 126
Applesauce 128
Apple Scalloped Potatoes, Char-
   lotte Shelton's 129
Apples, Fried 130
Apple Toddy, Tom Burford's 125
Asparagus and Eggs au Gratin 38
Aspic, Lydia Daniel's Canned
   Tomato or Vegetable Juice 50

B

Baby Greens, Pear, Walnut and
   Blue Cheese Salad 87
Baskets 7
Beef Stroganoff 36
Beets, Delicious Simple 77
Black Bean and Corn Salad, Nina
   Pillsbury's 88
Blackberry Cobbler 103
Blackberry Cobbler, Caketop 104
Black-Eyed Peas 76
Brownies from Scratch, Jocelyn's
   48
Brownies, Joan Roberson's
   Delicious and Easy 110
Brown Rice 81

C

Caketop Blackberry Cobbler 104
Carrot Souffle 78
Cauliflower, Puréed 80
Charlotte Shelton's Apple Scalloped
   Potatoes 129
Cheese Straws 1

Cheesey Chicken Casserole 26
Chicken
   Cheesey Chicken Casserole 26
   Chicken a la King 22
   *Chicken and Green Chiles Casse-
      role 23*
   Chicken Curry 25
   Chicken Taco Soup 11
   *Jocelyn's Chicken Country Captain
      46*
   Lisa's Non-Recipe for Chicken 24
Chili, Leigh Giles's White Bean 14
Chocolate Brittle 112
Chocolate Cake, Mary's 109
Chocolate Fudge Pie, Mimi's 111
Chocolate Sauce 113
Chocolate Tarts, Sallie's 116
Chutney Cheese Paté 4
Cobbler, Blackberry 103
Cobbler, Caketop Blackberry 104
Cold Salmon and Good Sauce 28
Cookies, You-Can't-Stop-Eating-
   Them 108
Cornbread, Hot Water 97
Corn Chowder 18
Crab and Caper Salad, Jane White's
   66
Crab in Shells, Deviled 32
Crawfish (or Shrimp) and Sausage
   Chowder 16
Cucumber Soup 12
Curry Vegetable Dip 5

D

Delicious Simple Beets 77
Deviled Crab in Shells 32

E

Ellen's Sausage Chowder 17

F

Fried Apples 130
Fudge, Terry Tosh's 117

G

Gazpacho, White 12
Greek Salad 65
Grits, Weekday 82
Guacamole 6

H

Hot Water Cornbread 97

I

Ice Cream, Macaroon Bisque 114

J

Jane White's Crab and Caper Salad
   66
Joan Roberson's Delicious and Easy
   Brownies 110
Jocelyn's Brownies from Scratch 48
Jocelyn's Chicken Country Captain
   46
Jocelyn's Pear and Apple Salad 47
Judy's Bran Muffins 95

L

Leigh Giles's White Bean Chili 14
Lisa's Delicious (and Easy) Summer
   Squash 74
Lisa's Non-Recipe for Chicken 24
Lobster Dinner 30
Lydia Daniel's Canned Tomato or
   Vegetable Juice Aspic 50

Lydia Daniel's Spinach-Artichoke
   Casserole 51
Lydia Daniel's Spoon Bread 52

Macaroon Bisque Ice Cream 114
Macaroon Custard 115
Macaroons, Almond 107
Marion Farmer's Quick Red Beans
   and Rice 40
Mary's Chocolate Cake 109
Melanie's Shitake Mushroom and
   Prosciutto Pasta Dish 39
Mimi's Chocolate Fudge Pie 111
Mina's Tuna Steak 35
Mina Wood's Nicoise
   (or Lynchoise) Salad 67
Muffins, Judy's Bran 95

N

Nina Pillsbury's Black Bean and
   Corn Salad 88

O

Omelet, Scrambled 94
Orzo Salad 64

P

Paella Salad 63
Pancake, Super 96
Pasta
   Melanie's Shitake Mushroom and
      Prosciutto Pasta Dish 39
   Spaghetti with Shrimp & Spicy
      Tomato Sauce 34
Paté, Chutney Cheese 4
Pear and Apple Salad, Jocelyn's 47
Pear, Walnut and Blue Cheese
   Salad 87
Pickled Shrimp 3
Potatoes au Gratin 79
Potatoes, Charlotte Shelton's Apple
   Scalloped 129

Puréed Cauliflower 80

Raised Waffles 93
Red Beans and Rice, Marion Farm-
   er's Quick 40
Rice, Brown 81

S

Salad
   Greek Salad 65
   Jane White's Crab and Caper 66
   Mina Wood's Nicoise
      (or Lynchoise) 67
   Nina Pillsbury's Black Bean and
      Corn Salad 88
   Orzo Salad 64
   Paella Salad 63
   Pear, Walnut and Blue Cheese
      Salad 87
   Taco Bean Salad 89
Sallie's Chocolate Tarts 116
Salmon and Good Sauce, Cold 28
Salmon with Lemon 27
Sausage Chowder, Ellen's 17
Scalloped Tomatoes 71
Scrambled Omelet 94
Seafood
   Cold Salmon and Good Sauce 28
   Crawfish (or Shrimp) and Sausage
      Chowder 16
   Deviled Crab in Shells 32
   Mina's Tuna Steak 35
   Pickled Shrimp 3
   Salmon with Lemon 27
   Shad Roe 29
   Shrimp Bisque 13
   Shrimp Cooked in Beer 33
   Spaghetti with Shrimp & Spicy
      Tomato Sauce 34
Shad Roe 29
Shepherd's Pie 37
Shitake Mushroom and Prosciutto
   Pasta Dish, Melanie's 39
Shrimp Bisque 13
Shrimp Cooked in Beer 33
Shrimp, Pickled 3

Soup
   Chicken Taco Soup 11
   Corn Chowder 18
   Crawfish (or Shrimp) and Sausage
      Chowder 16
   Ellen's Sausage Chowder 17
   Leigh Giles's White Bean Chili 14
   Shrimp Bisque 13
   Split Pea Soup 15
   White Gazpacho 12
Spaghetti with Shrimp and Spicy
   Tomato Sauce 34
Spinach-Artichoke Casserole, Lydia
   Daniel's 51
Split Pea Soup 15
Spoon Bread, Lydia Daniel's 52
Stewed Tomatoes 72
Strawberry Shortcake a la Prescott
   105
Stroganoff, Beef 36
Summer Squash, Lisa's Delicious
   (and Easy) 74
Summer Vegetable Casserole 73
Super Pancake 96

T

Taco Bean Salad 89
Terry Tosh's Fudge 117
Tomatoes
   Scalloped Tomatoes 71
   Stewed Tomatoes 72
   Tomato Pie 75
Tom Burford's Apple Toddy 125
Tuna Steak, Mina's 35

V

Vegetable Casserole, Summer 73
Virginia Apple Pone 126

Waffles, Raised 93
Walnut and Blue Cheese Salad 87
Watercress Sandwiches,
   Al Chambers's Mother's 2
Weekday Grits 82

White Bean Chili, Leigh Giles's 14
White Gazpacho (Cucumber Soup)
   12
Wistar Nelligan's Apple Pie 106

Y

You-Can't-Stop-Eating-Them
   Cookies 108